THE KRAKOW GHETTO PHARMACY

TADEUSZ PANKIEWICZ

THE KRAKOW GHETTO PHARMACY

TRANSLATED FROM THE POLISH BY
Garry Malloy

Wydawnictwo Literackie

Chief editor
Anita Kasperek

Editor
Antonia Lloyd-Jones

Proofreading
Beata Śmietana, Dorota Dziewońska, Jessica Taylor-Kucia

Graphic design
Marek Pawłowski

Technical editor
Bożena Korbut

This book was printed with the use of
Ecco Book Cream paper 80 g, 2.0 vol

Printed in Poland
Wydawnictwo Literackie Sp. z o.o., 2016
ul. Długa 1, 31-147 Kraków
free helpline: 800 42 10 40
internet bookshop: www.wydawnictwoliterackie.pl
e-mail: ksiegarnia@wydawnictwoliterackie.pl
fax: (+48-12) 430 00 96
tel.: (+48-12) 619 27 70
Typesetting: Scriptorium „TEXTURA"
Printed and bound by: Drukarnia POZKAL

ISBN 978-83-08-05114-6

I DEDICATE THIS MEMOIR
TO MY COLLEAGUES,
IRENA DROŹDZIKOWSKA,
HELENA KRYWANIUK AND
AURELIA DANEK-CZORTOWA,
WHO, FOR THE ENTIRE DURATION
OF THE KRAKOW GHETTO'S
EXISTENCE, RISKED THEIR LIVES
TO BRING AID TO ITS INHABITANTS.

FROM THE AUTHOR

When the "Jewish district" first opened, I unexpectedly became one of its inhabitants, as the owner of the "Pod Orłem" pharmacy at No.18 Zgoda Square. As only one of the four pharmacies in the Podgórze district was located within the ghetto, this fact initially escaped the notice of the German authorities. Later, the Germans tried to remove me from the ghetto by offering me one of the pharmacies in Krakow which had previously been owned by Jews.

I did everything in my power to put off the German authorities' decision. This included employing the tried and trusted method of offering every form of bribe I could think of. For I understood only too well that the Germans would lose the war, and would destroy my pharmacy, and that I would have to return property that was not mine to its rightful owner or his family when the war ended. My conjecture turned out to be well-founded. My pharmacy would have shared the fate of every business or apartment in the ghetto during its liquidation — it would have been completely destroyed.

By playing for time and by a twist of fate I spent two-and-a-half years in the tragic little Jewish town.

For understandable reasons, I wrote down my recollections of these unforgettable and horrendous times once the liquidation of the Jewish district had already taken place.

Even while the ghetto still existed, many of its inhabitants repeatedly urged me to write a chronicle describing the "Jewish district", as I was the only Pole to live and work among them there, from its inception to its liquidation. From the windows of my duty room overlooking Zgoda Square, I witnessed the most horrific crimes perpetrated by the Nazis against the defenceless Jewish population.

I have checked second-hand stories many times to ensure that my accounts of them are as faithful as possible.

In writing this memoir, I merely wished to present a chronicle of events and to recollect the atmosphere and emotions we experienced during that grim period of widespread cruelty and hypocrisy.

PREFACE TO THE 2ND EDITION

It has been almost thirty-five years since *The Krakow Ghetto Pharmacy* was first published. I have often been asked why the book has never been reissued, given that it sold so well. I have also received letters from abroad about this. In "particular" circles I have been accused of being a Zionist sympathiser, and I have experienced unpleasantness from some of my fellow countrymen who were entirely wrong in their assessment of my activities and the duties I performed during the nightmarish period of the Nazi occupation.

My friends have often urged me to publish my memoirs from that period of working at the "Pod Orłem" pharmacy in their entirety. When the first edition came out, it was abridged and incomplete for various reasons. This edition has been expanded and is not identical to the first. It includes everything that was in the first edition, as well as a large number of supplementary passages and several newly written sections.

Today, when I look through the yellowing pages of my manuscript from the historical perspective of all these years, the events and issues come to life with the same intensity as they did then, and I can see every character who came through my pharmacy as if they were alive. How many of them are no longer alive, how many survivors have been scattered across the globe?

I have accepted numerous invitations and travelled to many countries. In 1957, I stayed in Israel for three months. In 1965, I was invited to New York, where I took part in many meetings organised by Polish Jews, at which I compared their experiences and accounts with my memoirs.

I also met many of my old friends from the ghetto when we appeared as witnesses at the various trials of war criminals in West Germany.

My memoirs do not aspire to be a historical work, though they may be seen as a contribution to the history of the occupation and of the martyrdom of the Poles and Jews. They are a reliable, genuine and contemporary account written immediately after the war ended, when the people and events were still fresh in my memory. I also made use of the loose notes I made during the occupation.

In my memoirs I also wished to record the time which was a nightmare for the Jews in the Krakow ghetto, as it also was for me and those who were working with me, who helped the Jews as much as they could, often saving the lives of people condemned to die.

The atmosphere in the ghetto was so peculiar, so unusual, that it is impossible to describe how and what the people — the mere shadows of people — who spent time in this "inferno" really felt and thought. I think *The Krakow Ghetto Pharmacy* may shed some additional light on how human beings behave and act when exposed to danger and terror, and when being exterminated, as well as how those responsible for their misfortunes behave. Perhaps it will offer some contribution to understanding the psychology of criminals and their victims.

I have resisted the temptation to add autobiographical commentary on my own experiences, and I have not endeavoured to provide even an attempt at any kind of synthesis. I have tried as faithfully as possible, sometimes naively perhaps, to describe what I saw with my own eyes, hence a rather digressive style.

The present edition has not only been expanded, but also enriched with photographs, which are an eloquent record of that period too.

I wish to thank my friends for the initiative and for the efforts they have contributed to the publication of this book. I would particularly like to thank my colleagues Fryderyk Nedela and Dr Józef Wroński.

[1982]

CHAPTER I

THE CREATION AND ORGANISATION OF THE GHETTO — A NEW LIFE — NEW FRIENDS

At the beginning of 1941, there was increasing talk about the establishment of a ghetto. A wide range of districts were being mentioned, and there was all sorts of speculation. The most commonly expressed view was that Kazimierz would be the future Jewish town, for reasons of historical tradition and because it already had the highest Jewish population. Some people thought Grzegórzki, a district situated on the river Vistula, was sure to be the location of the future ghetto, because the river would provide a natural border along one side and thus limit the length of wall required… economy before all.

On 3 May 1941, the newspaper *Krakauer Zeitung* published a decree issued by Otto Wächter (the Krakow District Governor), concerning the establishment of a so-called *Jüdischer Wohnbezirk* — a Jewish quarter — for health and security reasons. An area in the Podgórze district, on the far side of the Vistula, was designated for this purpose, and the boundaries which would separate the ghetto from the Aryan part of the city were marked out.

The deadline for all "Aryans" to leave the demarcated ghetto area, and for the Jews of Krakow (of 80,000, only 15,000 remained) to move in, was set for 20 March 1941.

People were stunned. None of those directly affected was prepared to believe the decision was final. Those with an active interest in the decree — namely the inhabitants of the Podgórze district — formed delegations, called meetings and submitted formal requests outlining a wide variety of reservations, such as the number and nature of larger and smaller factory buildings and machinery repair shops which could not be relocated for lack of suitable premises, and so on.

Among those to appeal was the parish priest of St Joseph's, Father Józef Niemczyński; this he did both in person and through the diocese. Establishing a ghetto within the boundaries stipulated in the *Krakauer Zeitung* would directly harm the interests of the Podgórze parish, as it would lose most of its congregation, who would be forced to move across the Vistula. Apart from that, it would make access to the church extremely difficult for many parishioners; in order to reach it from any of the streets to the south-east of the ghetto, such as Wielicka Street, Zabłocie Street or Płaszowska Street, they would have to take a much longer route around the entire ghetto.

However, the appeals, delegations, petitions and requests came to nothing. The Germans' response to every single one was always the same: "There are plenty of churches in Krakow. Just be glad none of them is situated within the ghetto walls, because then you would lose your entire congregation." The decision of the German authorities was final — the establishment of the ghetto in the place and at the time determined by the Nazis was an incontrovertible fact.

And so the migrations began. From daybreak until late into the evening, trolleys, furniture carts, farm carts and handcarts moved through the city streets, carrying people's belongings to their new homes. There was an incredible hurry, because the deadline was short and everyone wanted to get tolerable accommodation.

Each day was like the next — with the same complaints, the same haste and the same din, weeping and wailing; people fainted from exhaustion as they dragged handcarts loaded with their possessions a long way across the city. The face of Kazimierz changed with each passing day; its character, built up over hundreds of years, quickly began to disappear. Those leaving included families who had settled in the district centuries ago. Shops, restaurants and places of worship on which the years had etched deep marks were closed down. The original, characteristic images disappeared from the streets of old Kazimierz. Bearded Jews, with sidelocks, black gaberdines, yarmulkes, felt and fox-fur hats were no longer to be seen walking around the squares or chatting on street corners, gesticulating in their typical manner. Gone were the clusters of boisterous, shabbily-dressed children who used to run up and down the narrow streets, the courtyards of dirty tenement houses, the wooden porches and broad entrance halls. One could no longer buy any goods late in the evening, though formerly they had been easy to obtain from shopkeepers standing in front of their closed shops after hours.

Gone was the mysterious atmosphere and special charm of the dusky, deserted streets and alleys, which were no longer illuminated by the weak light of the street lamps. Gone forever were the wooden shelters covered with fir tree branches, built in courtyards, on balconies and porches to commemorate the Israelites' time in the desert. The sight of Jews praying on the banks of the Vistula at Rosh Hashanah was no longer to be seen, though fortunately it has been immortalised in paintings such as Aleksander Gierymski's famous *Feast of Trumpets*. Just as the Nazis wanted.

For the time being, the decree ordering all residents and their businesses to leave the ghetto district by 20 March 1941 did not include the larger factories and plants producing army supplies, the courthouse and the adjacent jail, and my pharmacy. My staff, consisting of three qualified ladies — Irena Droździkowska, Helena Krywaniuk and Aurelia Danek-Czortowa — and I were issued with passes to enter the ghetto.

The resettlement of the population was completed within the deadline set by the German authorities. My parents had to move outside the ghetto walls, as no "Aryan" was allowed to live inside it any more. The only exceptions were the prison guard at the courthouse (the court and jail were removed from the ghetto after the deportations of June 1942) and I, as I went on living in the duty room at the pharmacy. Once again, this fact

1. A group of Jews before the war

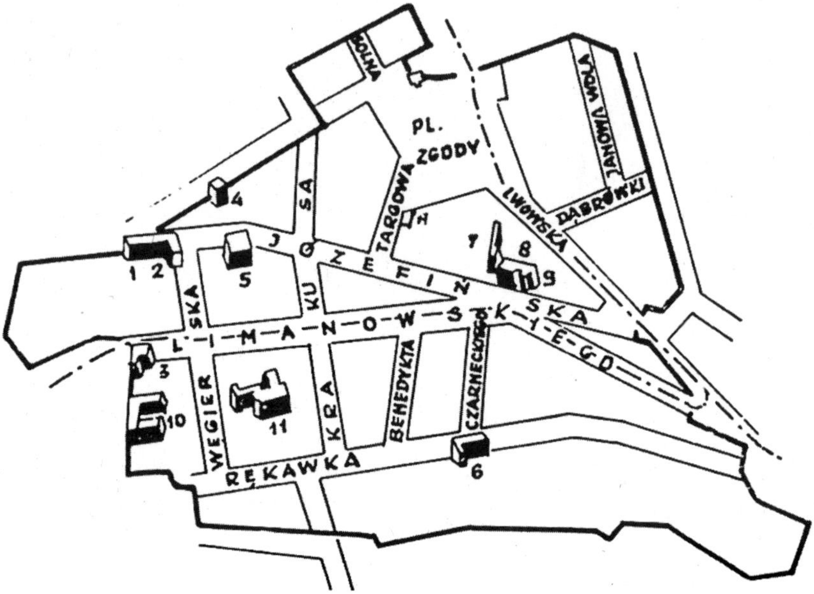

2. A map of the ghetto
in the first phase of its existence

escaped the German authorities' notice, and a little later was wordlessly sanctioned when the health authorities ordered a permanent night service at the only pharmacy in the ghetto. Destiny had placed the "Pod Orłem" ("Under the Eagle") pharmacy at the very heart of the ghetto, where it bore witness to the inhuman deportations, horrendous crimes and relentless degradation of human dignity perpetrated by the Nazis.

The ghetto included about three hundred and twenty tenement houses with a population of around sixty thousand inhabitants.

On 20 March 1941, I was alone in the pharmacy. At around 6 p.m. it suddenly started to get busy, and a few minutes later the place was so full that it was impossible to close the door. I soon discovered that there were German guards posted at the top of the streets leading out of the ghetto and that they were not letting anybody leave. People were upset and began passing comment. After a while they calmed down, telling each other an order must have been issued because of the Jewish Passover holiday, which had just begun that day. After closing the pharmacy at 8 p.m., I left the ghetto, wondering whether they would be willing to let me back in again. The German guard stopped me and inspected the documents permitting me to move about within the ghetto.

I asked whether I would be able to re-enter and received a terse "Nein!" in reply. However, at about 10 p.m. I came back. I was not on foot, but on the tram which ran through the ghetto, turning a broad arc into Limanowski Street. At the junction of Limanowski Street and Lwowska Street, I jumped off the moving tram, to the astonishment of the other passengers.

That was my first day in the closed ghetto.

Straight after Passover, the ghetto began to assume a strange new appearance. Dozens of labourers, builders and carpenters worked day and night, putting up walls, hammering in stakes, erecting gates and fitting bars to the windows of the tenements overlooking the Aryan district. People watched in horror as the walls rose up around them, built in the style of Jewish tombstones.

Finally, the whole place had been walled in, and all the windows had been fitted with bars. There were three gates leading into the ghetto. The main entrance was from Podgórski Square. This gate had two dark-blue lamps burning on either side and was topped with a large six-pointed Star of David and a big sign in Hebrew saying: "Jewish District". The tram ran through the centre of the gate and along the ghetto's main streets, Limanowski and Lwowska.

This gate was also the site of the main German police station and the headquarters of the *Judenrat* (the Jewish Council, created by the Germans to replace the existing Jewish *kehilla*). It was relatively easy to get hold of entrance passes here during the first few weeks of the ghetto's existence: the usual reason given was a need to collect money from the Jews.

The second gate was situated at the top of Limanowski Street, where it intersected Lwowska Street; the third gate led from Zgoda Square onto the third bridge over the Vistula. There were also Blue Police[1] stations at both of these gates. In general, most people came home from work via Zgoda Square. Here the Germans inspected documents and checked the amount of provisions being carried through; and through here a wide variety of goods were smuggled in at night.

The days and weeks went by. At first people watched in fear as the walls rose around them, which usually prompted bleak speculation: "Perhaps they'll try to starve us." I can still see the terrified face of a lady who often came to see me, accompanied by a wonderful dog. A close relative of Dr Bolesław Drobner, every day she would ask me: "Can you please tell me what people in Krakow are saying will become of us?" She suffered psychological damage which remained with her until the end of her time in the ghetto, in other words until the June deportation and her death in 1942.

Gradually, time was taking effect. People were getting used to life under these dramatically altered conditions and finding new ways of regarding their existence. Residents working in the city received a stamp in their *Kennkarten* (identity documents which replaced the former *Ausweise*) from the ghetto's newly opened

[1] The Blue Police (Polish: *granatowa policja*) was a popular name for the Polish Police of the General Government. Formed by the Nazis in 1939, this auxiliary police force was responsible for maintaining law and order in occupied Poland.

Arbeitsamt (or employment office). This entitled them to go out of the ghetto to their place of work. Each day thousands of workers passed through the ghetto gate with a *Kennkarte* in their hands and a white armband featuring a Star of David on their right sleeves. Thus the ghetto emptied in the morning and filled up again during the evening, up to the curfew at 9 p.m. Those who did not have permission to leave — including those who did not work in the city, children, the elderly and the sick — were left behind in the ghetto.

And so the days went by. Each day brought new decrees and new orders aimed at making people's unhappy lives even more difficult. The Jews' official representative body, the Judenrat — which was convoked by the Germans and comprised twenty-four members and a chairman, Dr Artur Rosenzweig — was based in Podgórski Market Square, in the same building as the main German police station. From its very inception, the Judenrat was answerable to the Gestapo. Issues relating to the ghetto were dealt with by Department III, in room 302 at No.2 Pomorska Street.

It was in this building that the cruellest crimes against the Jews were planned. This was the setting for interrogations, combined with beatings and torture. After the war, the cellars were found to contain human blood stains, nail marks scratched on the walls and holes made by bullets which had killed Poles and Jews alike.

The primary activity of the Judenrat was to carry out the orders of the Gestapo. It was also responsible for general administration, gathering statistics, taking censuses, registering shops, trying to procure food and fuel rations for ghetto residents, and editing, issuing and enforcing Nazi decrees. Over time, members of the Judenrat were obliged to perform ever harder and more unpleasant tasks.

A Jewish police force, called the *Ordnungsdienst* (OD), was formed, headed by Symche Spira. Dressed in a beautifully tailored uniform decorated with all sorts of insignia, Spira — a glazier by trade who wore a beard and a shabby old coat before the war began — suddenly became an important person. He was given the task of selecting men to form the uniformed Jewish police force, whose members were popularly known as "OD men". Distinct among them by uniform were the so-called *Zivilabteilung*, who wore V-necked jackets and ties, while the rest wore jackets that buttoned up to the neck. In both cases the right sleeve was trimmed with the word "Ordnungsdienst" written in Hebrew letters. The Zivilabteilung received special favours from the Gestapo.

In addition to blindly and ruthlessly executing Gestapo orders, the OD was also responsible for keeping order within the ghetto, exposing crimes, and implementing Judenrat directives. As time went by, the OD made life even more of a misery for the ghetto inhabitants.

Hospitals, orphanages and old people's homes were set up inside the ghetto. A Jewish post office was established on Limanowski Street, with its own Hebrew stamp for letters. There was also a small tax office, headed by a Mr Rajski. There was a bath house, and delousing and disinfection units. Clandestine classes in secular and Judaic studies flourished. Judaic classes were taught by the great Talmudist Lazar Panzer, and by Schein Klingberg, a leading expert on Jewish liturgy and mysticism. Klingberg was shot dead in Płaszów by a Gestapo officer named Strojewski. A dozen or so students attended music, drawing and painting lessons outside the ghetto walls, while the opportunity to leave it still existed on the strength of a pass. Well-known Krakow painter Professor Witold Chomicz gave many of these youngsters free classes at his home on Grodzka Street. Until his death in 1984, Professor Chomicz kept in touch with people to whom he had provided so much help and sympathy.

The ghetto's young Orthodox Jews belonged to an organisation called the "Talmud Torah". There were three synagogues, and religious life underwent very little change. Services were held and people generally continued to observe religious rules such as the Sabbath, holy days and fasting. Fervent piety was displayed during Jewish holidays: the tears and emotion on the faces of the faithful betrayed the intentions and content of their prayers only too well. From the windows of the pharmacy that looked onto a large courtyard, I saw some venerable old men with grey beards and sidelocks, clad in ceremonial robes, rocking steadily as they heeded the plaintive singing of the cantor. In every tenement in the ghetto, in almost every home, the prayer for the dead (or Kaddish) was feverishly being recited. I would see old Jewish women in embroidered lace shawls, standing stock still with glassy, immobile eyes as they listened to the monotonous chant of the prayer, frozen in pain and fear for themselves and their loved ones.

I often listened to conversations and debates about religious matters, particularly during the Jewish holiday periods. The serious, mystical mood of those gathered, further heightened by the semi-darkness inside the pharmacy, infected me with an irresistible energy. Those gatherings reminded me of Adam Mickiewicz's poetic drama *Forefathers' Eve*. Messianism was a recurring motif at those Jewish rituals.

A few years after the war I was visited by Father Karol Wojtyła, who would later become Pope John Paul II. Knowing that I had lived in the ghetto throughout its entire existence, he asked me the following question: "Do you perhaps know how the Jews viewed the subject of messianism during that dreadful period in the ghetto, faced as they were with brutality, murder and humiliation?" The question could only have been directed at me as an intermediate; the answer, however, could be given by nobody but an eminent Talmudist. I decided to get in touch with an expert in such matters, and I found the right man. He looked as if he had stepped straight out of a Gottlieb portrait, a dignified figure with long grey hair, piercing dark eyes and a patriarchal beard. He had a pensive, melancholy expression in his eyes.

3. An entrance gate into the Krakow ghetto

After listening to my question, he was silent for some time before turning his strangely enchanting gaze on me. With a gentle smile at the corners of his mouth, he spoke in a quiet, solemn voice: "The coming of the Messiah, yes…" — and here he paused briefly before continuing — "how can I explain it to you? You wouldn't understand it if I were to speak as I should… Try to imagine that after Friday comes Friday. Highly unlikely, isn't it? But not impossible. Allow me to put it differently. If there came a time when all the Jews the world over, every last man, woman and child, old and young, were simultaneously to refrain from sinning in thought, word and deed, then perhaps *that* might be the time, the time of the Messiah's coming, you understand? He may come, he will come one day… But you are unable to comprehend this." At this he gazed into the distance and, stroking his long, well-groomed beard, spoke in an ever quieter voice, as if to himself: "Friday after Friday, yet it can happen. We are waiting for that day, indeed we are." At this point he livened up again. "Yes, Mr Pankiewicz, it isn't a simple answer, it isn't so straightforward. But it's good you came, I'm glad you have visited me. Farewell."

The content of his reply, the atmosphere of that whole meeting, and the man himself — all of these things left an indelible impression upon me.

This rabbi, a just man, lived on Dietlowska Street, and the above-mentioned conversation took place at the Tempel synagogue on Miodowa Street. I took the liberty

4. A woman selling Star of David armbands
in the Krakow ghetto

of passing on the rabbi's response to the question of messianism to Father Wojtyła, who by then was a cardinal.

In those early days of the ghetto's existence, a friend of mine — a judge who was well-known for his trials and his good looks — would come to see me several times a month, always on a Saturday. Another person who took part in our meetings was one of the ghetto residents, an extremely pretty and fashionable lady with blonde hair and melancholy eyes, named Maryla Schenkerówna. With the blinds down and the lights turned off, we sat in my cosy room and in the glow of two small candles we ate Jewish-style fish brought from a nearby restaurant. After a few shots of plum vodka and a glass of white wine, it began to feel as if all was right with the world, just like in paradise. This mood lasted until the time came for my guests to leave. Brutal reality always left its destructive mark on those happy occasions. With his pass in his hand, the judge would leave the ghetto, and Maryla would quickly head home. Whenever there was unrest in the Jewish district, when people were being arrested and there was talk of an imminent deportation, Maryla would leave work (her job was in Krakow) and, instead of returning to the ghetto, would go to the judge's flat to wait for news. I would call round there at an agreed time with information about the present situation. Soon after the judge was arrested by the Gestapo and transported to Auschwitz, where he suffered terribly; beaten up and emaciated, with a broken arm, it is a miracle he survived the war. Miss Schenkerówna frequently dropped by the pharmacy to find out about the prisoner's fate. However, news from Auschwitz was very scant and generally untrue.

I also recall an extraordinary evening when my friend, Aleksander Kocwa — a professor at the Jagiellonian University — returned from the camp at Dachau and expressed his wish to see the ghetto. I sorted him out with a pass and, after a short walk around the streets of the enclosed district, I took him to the pharmacy. There we joined my work colleagues and some wonderful musicians (the renowned violinist Rosner, accompanied by his equally talented brother on concertina) in the duty room, where the blinds were lowered. In the glow of Sabbath candles, we all listened to the enchanting melodies of Viennese waltzes, ate from a table filled with Jewish delicacies, and completely lost all track of time. We forgot about the curfew, the war, the little walled-in town; and we forgot about the fate of all its unfortunate inhabitants who had been condemned to so much humiliation and tragedy. The supper lasted until the small hours of the morning. That was an unforgettable evening, and one which we fondly remembered many years after the war ended.

As time passed ever faster, people who until fairly recently could not have conceived how anyone could live in such conditions began to get used to them, giving up the most primitive needs of civilisation and slowly starting to forget their former lives. Worries about getting food each day, and struggles to keep jobs in the city which, although almost entirely unprofitable, at least offered the possibility of getting out of the ghetto, claimed the lion's share of everyone's free time. The Arbeitsamt, run by an Austrian named Schepessy, was open from morning until late evening. German, Polish and Jewish clerks were hired to compile records of those who had employment, to assign jobs, and to provide contingents of workers for labour outside the ghetto walls — in response to every demand from the German authorities.

Three times a week, the only Polish-language newspaper for Jews, *Gazeta Żydowska*, was delivered to the ghetto. It carried war communiqués announcing the latest successes of the invincible German army: "German victory on all fronts".

On the walls of the OD building, which was once a Catholic orphanage and later became an orphanage run by the Jewish "Centos" Society, the following slogan could be seen: *Deutschland siegt an allen Fronten.*[1] You can imagine the surprise of SS-Sturmscharführer Wilhelm Kunde, the Gestapo overseer of the OD, when one day he spotted that the "s" had been changed to an "l": *Deutschland liegt an allen Fronten.*[2] He pretended not to have noticed it; the poster was removed immediately, however.

1 "Germany is victorious on all fronts"

2 "Germany lies on all fronts"

Various small ads also began appearing on the walls of the town, and in the underground newssheet of the resistance, which bore the same name as a governmental publication: *Goniec Krakowski* (The Krakow Messenger). A mixture of malice and the macabre, these adverts aimed to ridicule and humiliate the Nazi invaders. We would read the following announcements:

"For sale: Jewish jewellery, blood washed off. Kommandant Amon Göth, Płaszów concentration camp".

"I can kill babies in the ghetto with one shot and sniff out a Polish conspirator even when I'm drunk. Joachim Thun, Bauinspektor, Prokocim barracks, Krakow".

"For sale: clothes, recently stolen by German swine. Heeresverpflegung, Krakau".

One of the first orders issued in the ghetto was for the immediate removal of all signs in Polish and for them to be replaced with signs in Hebrew. The only place this did not apply to was the pharmacy. The entire character of the ghetto was transformed. Those who were unacquainted with the Hebrew alphabet — a large number of people in the ghetto — suddenly felt as if they had stepped into a foreign country, where every notice, shop sign and nameplate consisted of incomprehensible squiggles. The order, as well as their enforced constant change of accommodation, proved to be most problematic of all for doctors, and had an adverse effect on their practice.

Economic life in the ghetto began to develop. New shops, restaurants, bakeries, dairies and eateries kept sprouting up like mushrooms after rain. There was even a restaurant-cum-dancehall with performances by local performers and an orchestra conducted by the aforementioned violinist Rosner and his brother.

Life in these new, decidedly unusual conditions went by at a dizzying pace. The constant tension and tough struggle to survive frustrated and demoralised the entire community.

From time to time, SS men walking through the ghetto would indulge their savage instincts by punching and kicking passers-by. The greatest humiliation was borne by the elderly, particularly those with beards and sidelocks. The SS men would drag them into the gateways, where they would shear their beards, chop off their sidelocks and yank their hair. This entertainment was almost always accompanied by punching, kicking and the piercing shrieks of the tormentors. As a result of the increasing frequency of such incidents, the Judenrat issued an order which forbade the wearing of beards and sidelocks. The most religious men, unwilling to part with their facial hair, got around the prohibition by wrapping scarves round their heads so that only their eyes and noses were visible. The day after the order was issued, the ghetto appeared to have been hit by a toothache epidemic — there were dozens of people walking around with their faces bandaged. Loyalty to tradition proved stronger than orders and threats. In the ghetto's early days, events like those caused a great deal of sensation and the residents' outrage knew no limits. And yet the pessimists had already begun to make ominous predictions about the future.

The number of Jews being beaten at work grew and grew, as did the frequency of SS attacks. The SS men would lie in wait on the bridge leading back into the ghetto, ready to pounce on workers returning home. I once witnessed the following scene which took place right outside my pharmacy.

It was around ten o'clock in the morning. A motorcar came speeding down the street and stopped in front of the pharmacy. There were two civilians sitting in the car; I moved closer to the door and recognised one of the men as Gustav Beckman, a Gestapo officer who was well known in the Podgórze district. Before the war, he was familiar to the people of Krakow as the owner of the "Toledo" razorblade factory. He was a thoroughly repulsive individual, and thus a fine specimen of the typical Nazi. Stocky, bullnecked, with a fat belly and an amorphous head, this poster boy for criminal atavism had become the monster of Podgórze. Sentenced to a year in prison before the war for insulting Poland, he later took his bloody revenge on the public prosecutor, Andrzej Bieńkowski, and the trial judges in the case, Władysław Bobilewicz and Konrad Frąckiewicz. Beckman called out to a Jew who was passing by the open car window. The man approached and, seeing the fat German with a swastika in his lapel, he immediately removed his hat. At that moment, the German punched him with full force in the face, and then drove off with a diabolical grin.

Such were the living conditions during the first months of the ghetto's existence. And somehow people began to get used to them, and to regard every savage event as perfectly normal and understandable.

And time was passing, bringing an uncertain future, which for obvious reasons with each new day seemed sadder and sadder. The ghetto had its fair share of optimists too, who believed that nevertheless… that perhaps it was possible to endure these conditions in some way. Throughout the entire existence of the ghetto, they firmly believed that the war would end any minute, and that Germany's defeat was inevitable. They believed that at any moment America, Britain, France and Turkey would take decisive action, that there was sure to be an invasion and that liberation would come any day now.

According to most people's definition, the pharmacy was like an embassy, a diplomatic post representing a world that was free in its own special way within this barred, walled-in town. It became a daily meeting place for many kind and fascinating people. This was where people of all walks of life and ages would meet regularly, where from early morning they would read the German and underground press, comment on the latest war communiqués, assess the political situation and discuss their daily problems and concerns. Here until late at night people held discussions, deliberated and made predictions. "Let something happen now," they would say. This cruel time seemed to have halted, as if the clock of history had stopped at a fatal hour. The hour of extermination.

The "Pod Orłem" pharmacy was one of two businesses in the ghetto to employ Poles. The other was a company producing optical lenses, which was situated on nearby Targowa Street (at No.6). Its manager was a well-known PPS[1] activist named Feliks Dziuba, who also ran "Spektrum", a company which produced glass for clocks and car windows, and which had its head office far beyond the ghetto walls. As both of these companies worked for the army, it was relatively easy for Dziuba to obtain ghetto passes for himself and for people employed at his glass factory. He and his workers — who included Wanda Kłosowa, Józef Mika and Tomasz Perski — commendably added their names to the list of those who brought assistance to the Jews. Feliks Dziuba managed to get Schepessy, head of the Arbeitsamt at the time, to assign jobs at "Spektrum" to dozens of Jews. These Jews were passed off as specialists, though none of them had any experience in the field. And Feliks Dziuba did not really employ them as such; he simply allowed them to while away a few peaceful hours there until it was time for them to return to the ghetto. Not much time went by before the news that Scheppessy had issued the passes reached the ears of the Gestapo, through their informer, Marcel Grüner. Schepessy was arrested and a few weeks

1 *Polska Partia Socjalistyczna* (Pol.) The Polish Socialist Party.

later he was shot. Dziuba and his colleague, Józef Zając, managed to get Benjamin Halbreich — a member of the ŻOB[1] — out of the ghetto and to employ him at "Spektrum". The optical lens factory operated from early in the morning until evening. The factory stopped working during German actions within the ghetto, and was closed shortly before the ghetto ceased to exist, at the time when it was controlled exclusively by the Gestapo. The company resumed production after the ghetto was liquidated. Feliks Dziuba also gained renown as one of the few people to have rescued pieces of the Grunwald monument on Matejko Square after it was blown up.

The year 1941 was drawing to a close. On 27 December, cars with loudspeakers mounted on their roofs entered the ghetto and informed the inhabitants that, in accordance with an order issued by the Stadthauptmann, all Jews were to surrender their fur coats and other items made of fur, without any exception, to the authorities at the Judenrat building at No.2 Limanowski Street. At the same time notices were posted to this effect, threatening severe penalties for resisting, including death. Later, the death penalty was the only punishment that came into account for failure to obey the Nazis' orders. From dawn till dusk, people queued for hours in the frost and snow to fulfil the order. Some people, unwilling to hand over

1 *Żydowska Organizacja Bojowa* (Pol.) The Jewish Combat Organisation.

their fur coats to the Germans, destroyed them at home by cutting them up into little pieces, burning them or burying them in the cellar. Others, who had no wish to wait in an exhausting queue, yet were afraid they would be caught destroying their fur coats, threw them on the ground and covered them with snow. There were also cases of people throwing their things into open cellars. The owners of these cellars later paid a heavy price for this — during the subsequent police searches, they were accused of concealing these items. That day there was a boom in smuggling and selling furs for a pittance.

The twenty-eighth of December 1941 was a Sunday. From early morning, German policemen had been conducting thorough searches. They searched houses, flats, attics and cellars; they peered into stoves to check whether fur coats had been burned in them. This in-depth search included the pharmacy. The Germans simply couldn't understand that I didn't own a single fur coat. I was sure that even if I had had such a thing, they'd have taken it off me. People used blankets to line the inside of their coats once the fur had been removed. The women used wool to embroider patterns onto their coat lapels so that they looked exactly like Crimean lambskin. Despite the severe misery suffered as a result of this action, it also gave rise to a good number of jokes at the Germans' expense. There were caricatures at the time of German soldiers shivering from cold at the Russian front, wrapped in women's fur coats and with Jewish fox fur hats on their heads.

It was New Year's Eve, 1941. The atmosphere in the pharmacy was convivial, with plenty of handshakes and good wishes. Towards the evening, the place was teeming with guests and we all forgot about the worries and problems of daily life. After all, there was alcohol in the pharmacy. We drank it in small amounts, and some believed that it made time pass even more quickly.

Some of the people who used to visit me were exceptionally intelligent and interesting, and the topics of conversation were highly diverse, including music, literature, pre-war politics and predictions for the future. My colleagues would bring in underground newspapers which were read with much interest; however, the underground press was met with incredulity inside the ghetto, not like outside.

A regular visitor to the pharmacy was Filip Schor, a former legal agent for a bank in Vienna and a man who knew the arias of every opera and operetta ever written, even though he didn't have a good singing voice. His simply phenomenal musical talent and perfect pitch never failed to impress. All you had to do was hum a melody more or less successfully and he could complete it, tell you who composed it and the year it was written, and quote its origins. A gifted erudite and polymath, Schor was also endowed with a prodigious memory and a broad range of interests, and was famous for his razor-sharp wit. He spent whole nights at the pharmacy whenever the residents received prior warning that the OD was carrying out a nocturnal round-up. On more than one occasion we watched through a crack in the pharmacy door as the OD men arrested the people on their lists and led them away from the tenements.

The German police patrol — which predominately comprised Viennese officers — often called in at the pharmacy, lured by the light shining through the blinds. They took part in the conversation and we offered them vodka so they'd lose interest in anyone whose presence in the pharmacy at such a late hour would have defied convincing explanation. They talked about Austria and reminisced about the Kaiser and Vienna in days of yore, and every discussion began and ended with the tunes of Strauss' waltzes. I must admit that these Viennese policemen always conducted themselves entirely properly towards the Jews they encountered at my place; they always addressed them as "Sir" and they chatted to them as though they had never heard of discrimination towards the Jews.

An ever-present member of our circle was M. Izraeler, who valued and traded in diamonds, and who had worked abroad for many years as a diamond cutter. Our friendship began in a quite remarkable way. In the first few weeks of the ghetto's existence, he would come to the pharmacy nearly every day for his medicine. As he waited for his prescription to be made up, he would read the newspapers and chat to one of my colleagues, Irena Droździkowska. One day he appeared and announced that he had a great favour to ask of her: he wanted to know if she would accept a gold medallion with an image of the Virgin Mary on it. From that day on we became steadfast friends and remained so until the very end. He was a man of impeccable character, a model husband and father. He would show up at the pharmacy at around ten o'clock each morning, take the latest issue of *Krakauer Zeitung* fixed to a cane for the readers' convenience, and silently immerse himself in his reading for an hour or so. After that came the commentary, discussion and predictions that the war was nearly over. Izraeler was one of those improbable optimists. He and his lovely wife, Anna — a slender woman with dark brown hair who was always neatly dressed — had a charming daughter called Dorina, who had fair hair and big blue eyes. They really were the perfect example of a loving family.

Izraeler and his extremely beautiful sister, Mrs Gutmanowa, were deeply devoted to their work at an old people's home, where they did all they could to relieve human suffering. Mrs Gutmanowa also looked after children at the Kinderheim on Józefińska Street. Her defenceless little charges were shot dead before her eyes. Fate did not permit Izraeler to see the end of the war; he perished, killed by a German bullet. Always clad in black, Anna and her daughter Dorina survived the occupation and, together with Mrs Gutmanowa, they emigrated to the United States. Gutmanowa's daughter, Anna Sislow, was waiting for her in New York. Anna Izraeler and her daughter went through very hard times as refugees. The fine and noble Izraeler family remained forever fixed in our memory.

A frequent visitor and extremely close friend of ours was Gizela Fendler (or Giza), a strong brunette with a dark complexion, always elegantly dressed. Before the war she was a member of the social elite in Krakow. It seems she was one of the first women to own a beautiful deluxe car and a gallery of valuable paintings. She had a remarkable talent for coping in the most difficult and seemingly hopeless situations, a talent which at times bordered on bravado. The following incident is a wonderful example of her extraordinary courage and composure.

When she was suddenly forced to vacate the vast flat in Krakow in which she was born and had spent the brightest moments of her formative years, Giza Fendler left a safe behind. The safe had an additional secret compartment built into it which could only be found by those in the know. And it was in this secret hiding place that Giza kept her precious jewellery and a considerable amount of dental gold (her husband was one of Krakow's best known and most sought-after dentists). When the Germans took over her flat, they left behind the old housekeeper who had lived with Giza for years. One rainy autumn evening, Giza knocked on the door of her former home. The door was opened by her old nanny, Hela Kohan, who was speechless, as if about to go into nervous shock.

"For the love of God, what are you doing here? You need to get out of here right away. The Germans are drunk, they're wandering all over the flat, and if they see you here, they'll kill you."

"Not another word," said Giza, putting a finger to her lips. "Go quietly and find out what they're doing and what state they're in."

No sooner had Hela left than Giza slipped into the dark room where her safe was kept. She opened it, removed the entire contents of the secret compartment and slowly made her way downstairs. A few seconds after she had faded into the darkness of the stairwell, the front door opened and one of the Germans dashed down the stairs, passing her on the way.

Giza pulled other admirable stunts as well. A few weeks after the Germans entered Krakow, she turned up at the office of the Stadthauptmann to ask for permission to withdraw the objects she had deposited in a safe at the PKO bank. One of the German authorities' first edicts involved freezing all bank accounts and blocking access to safety deposit boxes. The Stadthauptmann fell for Mrs Fendler's charms; as she spoke fluent German, he presumably took Gizela for a German who had been living in Poland for years and thus had Polish citizenship. Not only did he give her permission, but he also acquiesced to Giza's request that his clerk go with her to the bank. To the amazement of the bank's newly appointed managers, Giza showed her documents — which were supported by the explanations of the clerk accompanying her — and calmly opened her safety deposit box, removed its contents, handed the bank manager the key, then left. Gizela and her beloved son, Adam, survived the ghetto and the occupation and then left Poland for good, settling in America.

Several times a day, an older fellow pharmacist, Herman, would come to the pharmacy. Herman — an elderly gentleman with greyish hair and a kind smile — had worked as a pharmaceutical inspector in Lwów before the war. In the ghetto he was in charge of the sanitation department, a position which entailed wandering the streets all day with a cigarette permanently dangling from his lips. Whenever he was working in the vicinity, he would drop in, and he always had something interesting to say, whether it was about political developments or news to do with the ghetto. During one of the deportations, he disappeared from the ghetto and was never heard of again.

One voice of sober realism during our daily political discussions at the pharmacy belonged to Natan Oberlender, a well-known lawyer in the Krakow area. He believed the war would go on for at least six years, no less. He used to say: "This war must last at least as long as the last one, if not longer, which is why I give it six years".

This would provoke a storm of protest from E. Wachs, the owner of a lamp factory in Podgórze, who used to read the newspapers a second time "between the lines", interpreting every sentence in it as meaning that the Germans would inevitably be defeated: "After all, it's clearly written here, you just have to know how to read it". His one burning desire was to see his sons, who had gone

5. The "Pod Orłem" Pharmacy
at No. 18 Zgoda Square

east to evade the advancing German army in September, 1939. "This longing," he would say, "is so strong that it makes you capable of weathering the worst." His desire was never to be fulfilled; he was arrested on 28 October 1942, and perished like everyone else in that deportation.

Another daily visitor to the pharmacy was a doctor by the name of Roman Glassner, who was well-known in Krakow. He had a slight stoop, a head of grey hair and a permanent smile. Glassner was an extremely cultured man with an extensive knowledge; he was also a connoisseur of classical music. He would come to the pharmacy for a little glass of chartreuse and "the odd fairytale", as he put it. His innate cheerfulness and *joie de vivre*, which he maintained even in the ghetto, was destroyed when he was informed of the arrest of his daughter, whom he loved more than life itself. His daughter, Stanisława Skiminowa, was married to a doctor, the son of a professor at Krakow's Jagiellonian University. A wicked denunciation led to her arrest and separation from her husband. At first she was taken to Montelupich Prison for interrogation, and then later to the ghetto, where she was put in an isolation cell in the hospital on Józefińska Street. This is where they also held the mentally subnormal imbeciles who had been transferred from the hospital on Kopernik Street. The cell occupied by Stanisława Skiminowa was guarded day and night by a policeman from the Jewish OD.

Dr Glassner moved the proverbial heaven and earth to save his daughter, and to that end he spent what

6. Tadeusz Pankiewicz during the occupation

remained of his fortune. And then something that can only be described as miraculous occurred. Astonishingly, Stanisława managed to escape from the prison under cover of darkness. Her successful escape and the manner in which it was accomplished were thanks to two Polish women: Zofia Krzyżańska and Olga Kęplicz. Both women used their acquaintance with a Mr Förster — of whom I shall say more later — to save Poles and Jews in the ghetto.

One of the ghetto's most infamous characters was a sales representative named Marcel Grüner. He was tall, handsome and well-built, and was about thirty-two years old. He began visiting us frequently, trying to sell us various cosmetic products. A coward by nature, he aroused my suspicion. I didn't know what to make of him at first. His was constantly trying to find out how much people were earning, what their turnovers were and what kind of lifestyles they were leading. He was at the pharmacy every day, especially during the late evening, when he would often bring us various tasty treats. As everyone said, I had a huge influence on him and I was always able to get him to do what I wanted. One time it was about finding a place to stay for a woman named Kemplerowa who had no roof over her head. I managed to exert my influence on him, and he agreed to take the woman and her child in (he had two rooms). After some time he threw her out, allegedly because the child was sick. I called him all the names under the sun, saying that unless he took her back, I'd have nothing more to do with him. He came, apologised and allowed her to move back in.

People said that Grüner was working for the Germans, that he was too sure of himself, too much at ease in various situations. I once met him in town and he wasn't wearing the obligatory Star of David armband; I pretended not to have noticed. I decided to find out what he was doing for the German authorities. One evening, when he came to the pharmacy, we decided to ply him with alcohol and then search him. Despite his strong appearance and health, Grüner was a lightweight when it came to alcohol. He got as drunk as a lord and fell asleep like a baby. It turned out that his wallet contained a German informer's identification card, which entitled him to move around the streets of Krakow without an armband. After a couple of hours, Grüner woke up remembering nothing, said goodbye and left.

It later transpired that Grüner had initially worked for the tax and excise office, and had then been arrested by the Gestapo but, after three days, they had released him and he had evidently become a spy, officially at their service. He wasn't so much a bad man as an utterly stupid and submissive individual, and when the Gestapo skilfully put the screws on him he gave up dozens of Jews. From that moment on, our acquaintance with him pretty much came to an end. He realised that we knew about his role for the Gestapo, but he had enough self-respect to avoid acquaintances he was likely to run into at the pharmacy, so he kept his visits to a bare minimum.

If he did come by, he'd assure me that he'd be going abroad soon and that he'd write to me, and then I'd understand and no longer condemn him. I wished him the luck of having that happen as soon as possible. He never went; instead he continued in his dishonourable career right up until his well-deserved end. He and his wife were supposedly shot by a resistance organisation some time after March 1943. During the early period of our acquaintance, he complemented the aforementioned Schor wonderfully. He was extremely musical and a gifted singer, and he and Schor would give concerts, singing duets from some of the most magnificent operas and operettas.

Another regular customer and essential link in our chain of friends was Dr Leon Steinberg. Then there were Dr Władysław Sztencel and a charming pessimist named Freud, who looked like an old Polish nobleman with his handlebar moustache, gentle and jolly face, lively eyes and elegant hand gestures.

Freud was always smiling and content, as was his wife, Mrs Freud. He knew everything about everything; he also knew much about the world, which he had toured when he worked for the Polish consulate in Berlin.

The final link in the chain was Dr Armer, a man of impeccable character and an expert on the Talmud and Kabbalah. He came to me and asked if he could entrust to me for safekeeping twelve extremely precious Torah scrolls which had ended up in the ghetto. We were deeply saddened to hear that he had been shot at

7. Pharmacy staff in front
of the ghetto entrance (1942)

Płaszów concentration camp, which I will discuss in fuller detail later. He was the one who recommended to me two Poles who had ghetto passes because of their employment. Both of these gentlemen, Władysław Szałek and Roman Zbroja, reported to the pharmacy several times a month (and sometimes more often than that) with large envelopes containing various counterfeit documents, *Kennkarten*, newssheets printed by the underground press and expertly forged stamps for a variety of documents. The intended recipients usually came to collect their envelopes in the evening, or sometimes late at night. After our regular customers had finished reading the newspapers, they were passed on. Władysław Szałek had a secret printing press in his flat, which he ran with Zbroja and several others, including a well-known graphic artist from the ghetto named Henryk Teichler (who would disappear whenever he sensed the approaching deportations and find shelter at Szałek's place until the action was over).

Szałek and Zbroja brought their activities in the ghetto to an end when it came under the control of the Gestapo, i.e. on 15 October 1942, from which point all ghetto passes became invalid.

From time to time I received visits from a doctor of law and philosophy named Rappaport. Rappaport was a writer and a journalist, and a well-known figure in Lwów. A tall, grey-haired man of about sixty-eight, he lived in the ghetto with his aged sister. He was incredibly intelligent, and a pleasant and interesting speaker.

I enjoyed listening to him talk about his academic work, his travels and his observations and opinions of the world. Curiously, he was not in the least interested in the war, he didn't seem to care about news from the front or matters pertaining to the daily fight for survival. He lived his life as if he were on another planet, immersed in his books and academic problems. He was a mathematician by avocation and was always puzzling over some mathematical problem or another.

"I've never been bored in my life," he once told me, "even if I lived for a thousand years, I'd still have so many interests that I wouldn't have time for all the problems that engross me."

One time he came and revealed that he wanted to send a registered letter to Geneva, or to the Swiss embassy in Berlin, because — he claimed — he had solved a mathematical problem which Pythagoras had regarded as unsolvable, namely dividing an angle into three parts using a straightedge and a compass. He assured me he had done all the possible calculations and that he wasn't mistaken. I was unable to send his letter to the Swiss embassy in Berlin; I didn't tell Rappaport this because I didn't want to upset him. He came by each day to ask if there was a reply. He believed that the publication of this piece of work would make him a rich man, that the Germans would be sure to release him and his sister from the ghetto and that he would live as a free man. I told him that I knew a professor at the university, a mathematician, that I'd go see him and that I'd get

8. The staff of the "Pod Orłem" Pharmacy.
From left: Helena Krywaniuk, Aurelia Danek-Czortowa,
Tadeusz Pankiewicz, Irena Droździkowska

him a ghetto pass, so that the two of them could meet at the pharmacy to discuss the subject. He was very enthusiastic about my proposal and the meeting did indeed take place. My friend, Tadeusz Ważewski, a renowned professor of mathematics at the Jagiellonian University, told me from the outset that the problem definitely had no solution, like the concept of perpetual motion, but that he would be pleased to visit the ghetto and talk to Dr Rappaport. In fact, they met twice.

After checking Dr Rappaport's work thoroughly, Professor Ważewski said that even though the problem could not be solved completely, the method provided by Dr Rappaport was one of the best and most accurate of all the existing methods, and it would be published in academic journals. This did happen after the war, but Rappaport never saw the fruits of his labour; he died after being deported during the operations of June 1942.

We had some interesting chats with Abraham Neuman, a painter who was renowned both in Poland and abroad. He had travelled the world and had spent a good deal of time in Paris, where exhibitions of his work met with considerable acclaim. He was undoubtedly an extremely talented artist and an exceptional individual. Despite his advanced age, he was blessed with a passionate personality and an unquenchable *joie de vivre.*

In the ghetto he lived very modestly, but he adamantly believed things would be better, and that he would rejoin the world outside. He was bound to survive the Germans and their defeat. He did relatively few paintings in the ghetto; in order to make some money, he did portraits from photographs and charged a pretty penny for them. This was because he assumed that if somebody wished to approach such a renowned artist just to have a photograph enlarged, then so be it: but the ignoramus (his words) would pay through the nose for it.

"For the same amount of money I can make your wife look thirty years younger, if you like," he would say, "and you wouldn't even have to bring me a photograph of her."

Filip Schor was there when he said this and interrupted: "Forgive me for interrupting you, but I have a little tale to tell you which I'm sure you'll find rather apt."

Neuman went quiet for a moment and, glancing at him suspiciously, said: "Go ahead, but be quick. I'm sure whatever story you concoct will be ridiculous."

Schor began: "You know, there was once a painter, one of those fashionable artists of yours, who was commissioned by an old peasant woman to paint a portrait of her late husband. The woman's husband had died just three days before. As the old woman didn't have a photograph of him and the artist had never seen him, she had to describe the deceased as best she could: what he looked like, his eyes, his nose, his mouth, his forehead, and so on; the painter took out a sheet of white paper and wrote down everything the grieving widow said. 'It'll be ready for collection in ten days,' said the artist. Ten days passed and the woman knocked at the artist's door. He sat her down in front of an easel with the painting on it — the painting was covered with a dark cloth. 'Look carefully,' said the painter, gazing hypnotically into the woman's eyes. 'Look carefully,' he repeated, this time more forcefully, and approached the painting. The old lady didn't move an inch. One, two, three... with a single sudden movement the artist whipped the cloth from the painting... The old widow shuddered, she looked and looked, she stared goggle-eyed at it, her mouth agape, and then clutched her head and cried: 'My God! It's only been two weeks since he died, and look how much he's changed, the poor thing! I hardly recognised him — who'd have thought it, eh?'"

Schor stopped and patted Neuman on the shoulder. Neuman gave him a nasty look, told him obscenely where to go, and then sat down to drink a cup of warm tea. He didn't utter another word, in spite of our entreaties.

"Some other time, when that buffoon isn't here."

Schor remained jovial; he had a great sense of humour, wasn't easily offended and always emerged from verbal skirmishes as the victor, seeing the funny side in everything.

Neuman was interested in palmistry and on his visits he would read palms and facial features, guess the past and predict the future. And it has to be said, he was very good at it. He had the gift of narration and was a keen and interesting speaker. The only thing he complained about was his bad relationship with the woman he lived with — because he made her pose in the nude for him. And because the poor woman was somewhat plain and getting on a bit (she was about sixty), it came as no surprise to hear that those sittings always ended noisily and tempestuously.

I recall a charming evening I spent at the pharmacy in Neuman's company. He arrived with Mordechai Gebirtig, the celebrated Jewish folk poet. Gebirtig recited his charming verse *S'brent* ("It is burning"). Two years later it became the battle song of the Warsaw Ghetto Uprising. Jewish insurgents fought and died to the strains of that song. I can still hear the melodic whisper of the poet's words: *zun, zun, zong*. They had a lyrical, dreamlike quality. "This poem was written with tears," he told me, "because I cried like a baby when I was writing it." Gebirtig was killed by a German bullet during the deportation of October 1942.

Another regular visitor to the pharmacy was Dr Abraham Mirowski, the distinguished Krakow ophthalmologist. Mirowski was a highly regarded expert and a skilled surgeon. Ever cheerful, he was a calm and tactful man; yet sadness and reverie were never far away. He showed up in the ghetto in February 1942. After he arrived he found out that his wife had died. Following his wife's death, his son was kindly taken care of by a Mr Ameisen and his wife, Mrs Ameisen-Dietlerowa. Some time later, Dr Mirowski's little boy was taken away by the Germans and was never heard of again. Despite his father's relentless efforts to find him, nothing was discovered of the boy's fate; but the kind-hearted Dr Mirowski never stopped believing that his son was alive, and he continued to await his return.

Dr Mirowski remarried in the ghetto. The ceremony took place on 6 May 1943, and was conducted by a fortuitously identified rabbi who had wanted to keep his occupation a secret. People shut in the ghetto were very keen not to be alone, and they were very keen not to be deported alone or to die alone. After the war, the Mirowskis moved to Israel and settled in Haifa. I paid them a visit there when I spent several months in that country in 1957.

One of the ghetto's most mysterious characters — and yes, such characters did exist there — was Aleksander Förster, whom I mentioned earlier when I talked about Stanisława Skiminowa's escape from prison. Förster, reportedly the son of a piano maker from Leipzig, was a German Jew who spoke broken Polish with a chronically hoarse voice. He was about forty years old, of average height, black-haired but going bald, and always well-dressed. His hips swayed gently as he walked. He wore a large signet ring but no Star of David on his arm. He spoke several languages, had travelled the world and before the war he managed a group of dancers. I met him in August 1939, when he was in Krakow with an English dancer who was appearing at the "Feniks" club. Right after the ghetto was established, people began saying that Förster had played an important role as a spy for the Germans. And that's why he made the most of the tremendous privileges this brought, namely being allowed to walk around the ghetto and outside it without an armband. He also had a three-roomed flat all to himself, which was located just next to the ghetto entrance; in the same building he ran a restaurant-cum-dancehall, which he later leased.

He took advantage of his right to enter or leave the ghetto at any time of day or night, regardless of the curfew. He had a second flat in Krakow, at the Royal-City Hotel. He was allowed to greet Gestapo officers with a raised arm, and they in turn greeted him with a handshake; he was on first-name terms with many of them and he would organise parties for Gestapo dignitaries of various ranks. Those festivities would often last well into the night, and sometimes until morning — on their way home his guests would remind the ghetto's inhabitants of their existence by firing their pistols. It was even said that Förster had his own office in the Gestapo's main building on Pomorska Street and that he sat there in a German uniform (how much of this was true is uncertain). It was also widely said that the Gestapo had him prepare their so-called *Stimmungsberichte*, i.e. reports concerning the public mood. He showed more of himself during the deportations and while stamps were being issued for leave to remain in the ghetto. Many people tried to get close to him, believing in the efficacy of his intervention. And, as it turned out, Förster's capabilities were indeed great. He was able to get stamps for a good number of people who would otherwise never have been permitted to remain in the ghetto. During the deportation operations in June, I saw Förster moving about freely among

Gestapo officers of every rank. On Zgoda Square he intervened for some Jews (often for no personal gain) and got them out of the transport.

One day the ghetto was electrified by the news that Förster had been arrested and imprisoned in the OD jail the night before, following a Gestapo order that came by telephone. The next day some Gestapo officers arrived at the ghetto, where one of them, a chap named Hermann Heinrich, went to the OD and ordered them to open Förster's cell. After some time, Heinrich and Förster emerged from the cell in high spirits, laughing and joking. I was told by Bousko, the man who later became the *Schupo*[1] chief for the Podgórze district (and whom I will mention later), how the arrest came about. Hermann Heinrich was celebrating his promotion in the Gestapo building on Pomorska Street. Among the many gifts he received was a large basket of red roses and a congratulatory note from Förster. For a joke, Heinrich called the OD and ordered them to arrest Förster. Apparently, this was his way of making sure Förster knew that, in spite of everything, there was a marked difference between them — that he was a representative of the *Herrenvolk* and that Förster was of Jewish origin and, thus, an *Untermensch*.

Two events happened in the ghetto which clearly showed that the Germans showed no consideration for

1 *Schupo (Schutzpolizei)* (Ger.), lit. "protection police", the German municipal police force which was responsible for keeping order in towns and cities.

anyone, not even those who were blindly devoted to them: when the Gestapo put Förster in jail, and when the head of the OD, Spira, was punched in the face by SS man Horst Pilarzik.

When it comes to what went on inside the ghetto, you couldn't — in my opinion — accuse Förster of any wrongdoing. Whether he intervened for money, gifts, or for selfless reasons (because there were incidents of this kind too), he managed to save people from deportation and, on more than one occasion, he even facilitated their escape.

After the liquidation of the ghetto on 13 March 1943, Förster lived in Krakow. He went on a mission to Hungary and came back after three weeks. He was suspected of collaborating with British intelligence... He left again, but was arrested upon his return and sent to Montelupich Prison. He vanished without a trace. We knew only that he had been eliminated. After some time, Gestapo officers began spreading the rumour that the charge which had led to Förster's imprisonment had turned out to be false. As a result — they said — they had released him and sent him on an espionage mission to Britain. Yet another German lie.

I once received a letter from the United States, from the aforementioned Rosner brothers. In the letter they informed me that they had been talking to a man who was in prison with Förster at Montelupich, and who had seen the Gestapo beating Förster to death with clubs.

In the first few days after the ghetto was established, an interesting woman named Dora Schmerzler turned up at the pharmacy. She was a German Jew who had defected from Germany during Hitler's rise to power in the 1930s. In Krakow she worked at the Aleksandrowicz paper company on Długa Street. Schmerzler was an attractive lady: shapely, impeccably dressed, with a creamy complexion, sapphire-blue eyes and reddish hair, the ideal Rachela from Wyspiański's play *The Wedding*. She left the ghetto during the deportations and returned after it was all over. During the June deportation, she came to say farewell before she left, telling us she would drop by the pharmacy in a few days. But because she was absent from the ghetto, she was unable to receive a blue card, or *Blauschein*, which entitled the holder to remain within the ghetto walls. So she left Krakow and moved to Zabierzów, where she lived with a small group of Jews in hiding, who were being helped by a kind-hearted gentleman called Dr Bieżyński. Dora's guardian angel was a younger colleague of mine named Artur Biberstein, who was goodness itself. He worked miracles to get Dora a stamp on the relevant document, and to get her a blue card which entitled her to stay in the ghetto. After some time, he had got Dora all the necessary documents and she came back. We found out that two days after Dora left Zabierzów, the Gestapo arrested all the Jews with whom she had been hiding and executed them. Among the victims were Ignacy Ganger and Ignacy Bober, both of whom had facilitated

Dora's correspondence with Artur Biberstein while she was staying in Zabierzów, and who had been active beyond that area too.

One time Artur was searched by the infamous Rottenführer Ritschek, who found a letter Artur had begun writing to Dora. Ritschek beat Artur up and arrested him. It looked as though Artur was done for, but a sudden intervention at the office of Sturmscharführer Kunde led to his release. The man who intervened and saved Artur was Dr Weichert, in whose office Artur worked. There was probably nobody in the ghetto who could talk to the Germans as Dr Weichert could. He knew them incredibly well, he knew their mentality and their way of thinking. Many people owed their lives to him without even realising it.

From time to time we were visited by Dr Romuald Lachs, a urologist and an excellent surgeon. This tall and well-dressed gentleman spoke slowly and thoughtfully; he gave the impression of a man who was constantly working to solve some problem or another. As for the matter of the Jews in the ghetto and the fate that awaited them, his view remained the same from the outset. "They'll die, they're bound to die, it's obvious — all you have to do is look at what's happening around you. For the time being I'll wait," he said, "but I'm not going to meet my end here." The day before one of the deportations, Dr Lachs disappeared, but nobody could say for certain what had happened. It later turned out that he and his family had managed to reach Warsaw. There he was taken prisoner during the Warsaw Uprising and, along with some other fighters, was driven ahead of the German tanks as they drove at the insurgents' barricades. He died a hero.

A diverse range of personalities continually came through the door of the pharmacy. For example, Wiktor Kepler, who worked at the hospital in the department of internal diseases. He was a tall man aged forty-five, with a slight stoop and a drooping head. He had large dark eyes, and his smile looked as though it had been glued onto his face. He spoke in a low voice, dragging out every word, and he always looked you straight in the eyes when he spoke to you. He never sat down, preferring to stand while chatting, and his oft-repeated mantra was: "As for what will become of us, *ich sehe schwarz*". Not wishing to be separated from his wife who had been assigned to the March deportation, Kepler voluntarily went with her. One of the Germans saw him at the assembly point and pulled him out of the crowd. Kepler wound up in Płaszów concentration camp, and was later transferred to another camp in Szebnie. He was shot during the liquidation of the camp, just before the end of the war.

Then there was Dr Jan Lachs, an associate professor at the Jagiellonian University. This seventy-three-year-old gynaecologist was still active despite his advanced age; he eagerly performed operations, all of which were successful. An eminent expert in the history of medicine, he could usually be found poring over old volumes containing nuggets of medical wisdom from centuries past. His recommended method for effectively making it impossible to tell that a ritual operation had been performed was generally known and practised in the ghetto.

A few times during the ghetto's existence, Salomon Spitzer turned up at the pharmacy. He taught classes in Jewish theology at the secondary school in Podgórze (which I attended) and was also an eminent orientalist.

And finally, I must mention the well-known and widely respected Dr Aleksander Biberstein, who ran the isolation hospital in the ghetto. At first the hospital was situated on Rękawka Street, and then it moved to a little blind alley off Zgoda Square. Dr Biberstein was an outstanding diagnostician, a superb organiser and community worker, and a wonderful human being; years before the war began, he was famous not only in the Podgórze district, but also in the whole of Krakow. He lived in the ghetto with his wife and son. My friendship with Dr Biberstein predated the war by many years. And so it was somewhat unusual that we rarely saw each other in the ghetto. Or perhaps not so unusual, given that life was no longer normal. The perennial lack of time, the everyday struggle for existence and the huge workload experienced by every doctor (but especially Dr Biberstein) didn't create the kind of atmosphere necessary for leading a social life. For many years, right up until his departure for Israel, Biberstein held the post of director of the state-funded medical clinic in Krakow. I corresponded with him until the end of his life.

Many people came through my pharmacy in that period: friends, close friends, lesser acquaintances, and strangers. All of them were interesting in their own way. It would be impossible to list all the people here to whom I should devote at least a few lines of my memoirs. There were many undoubtedly fascinating people with whom, however, there was no opportunity for closer contact.

CHAPTER II

MOMENTARY PEACE… — THE FIRST DEPORTATION — GERMAN INFORMERS — THE DEPORTATIONS OF 2–4 JUNE 1942

Despite the heavy workload in the pharmacy (which for a period of almost two years consisted of constant day and night duty), time flew by in the company of my friends and acquaintances, many of whom were very dear to me. Together we shared the pains and worries of the ghetto residents, we took an active interest in each Nazi or local authority directive which affected the ghetto and its populace. After every important event, every deportation, the pharmacy was the first port of call for our friends. I was rarely alone there, particularly after the curfew. Out of fear of arrest, many people stayed the night there. They would leave the pharmacy in the morning through the door in the annexe. We were glad to see those who remained after every deportation. We would drink to good fortune, to drown sorrow and dull the pain of those touched directly by fate. And then we would find out who was gone, who was wounded, who had perished, who had lost their closest friends and family. Here we told each other about the acts of destiny, the miraculous coincidences and the luck or misfortune of various people. With great excitement each person described their mishaps and adventures, expressed their opinions on a great number of matters to do with the deportation, and criticised or praised individual OD men.

Occasionally non-Jews would drop into the ghetto. I should mention one of them, Dr Ludwik Żurowski, a doctor who, as a so-called local physician, had permission to enter the ghetto. Taking advantage of this entitlement, he used to bring the ghetto residents foodstuffs, mainly fats, and… he also made them look younger. Thanks to an appropriate hair dye, grey-haired old people, who were considered as unfit for work (and therefore were at particular risk of extermination), suddenly became *arbeitsfähig* — capable of work. Hundreds of litres of liquid to restore natural hair colour and hide the grey was sold from our pharmacy laboratory.

My school friend, a lawyer named Mieczysław Kossek, often visited the pharmacy. When I was gathering materials for my memoirs, he handed me his own account of the period, entitled "An Encounter at the Pharmacy". What follows is an extract from this account.

"The first time I found myself in the ghetto area was in 1941, on my way to the court in Podgórze. I was gripped by a strangely unpleasant feeling, seized by anxiety, sadness and a deep sympathy for the people who had to suffer so terribly there. I saw a small group of pale, emaciated children playing a game of hopscotch; at the sight of me — a stranger, perhaps a German — they stopped playing and watched me anxiously, waiting to see how I would behave towards them. I gave them a few sweets, which I brought with me to give to the secretaries

9. Tadeusz Pankiewicz's colleagues
in front of the pharmacy entrance

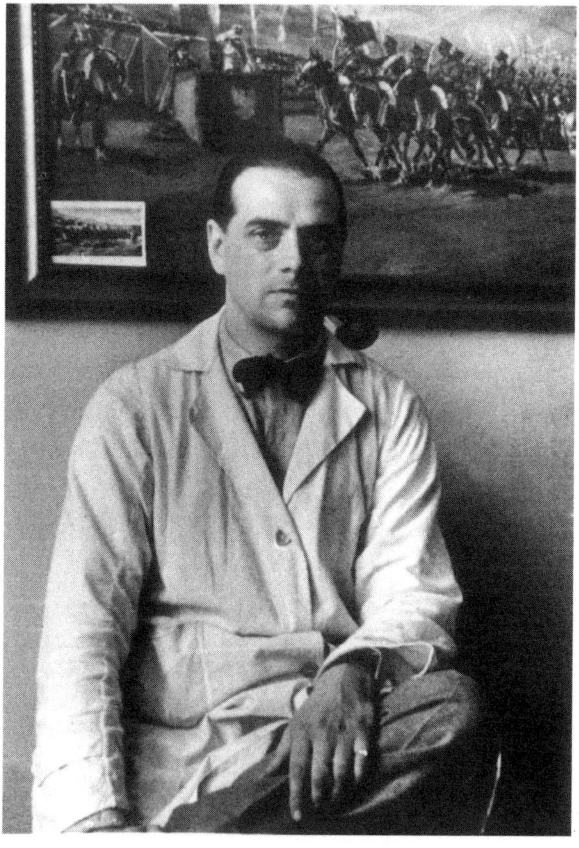

10. Tadeusz Pankiewicz in the back room
of the pharmacy

at the court. Then I left because the trial was about to begin. The courthouse was on Czarniecki Street in the ghetto area. I walked past the 'Pod Orłem' pharmacy but as I was in a hurry I didn't go in. Only once the trial was over did I go inside; I couldn't believe my own eyes when I saw my friend, Tadeusz Pankiewicz, standing there in a white coat. We talked for a long time.

"From that day on, I would drop by the pharmacy several times a week, whenever I had trials at the court. Other friends came there too, and we used to chat and share news from the BBC and the underground press.

"That was when we agreed to find ways to help get our Jewish friends out of the ghetto. Now and then I provided Pankiewicz with two or three civil court summonses, which would be grounds for the German guards to allow Jews to leave the ghetto.

"These summonses had authentic court record reference numbers written in by the court secretaries, Aleksandra Wysocka and Mieczysława Kobylarz. The space for the recipient's name was left blank, to be filled in later by Pankiewicz as required. Many people came out of the ghetto this way."

Antoni Wroński, a teacher in Podgórze, also used to come and see me on his way to or from the court. Before the war, he and Bolesław Taszycki — father of the famous linguist, Witold Taszycki — would come to the pharmacy almost every day to get herbal medicines from my father. A popular character in Podgórze, Professor Wroński was a good man. Nicknamed "Goatee

Beard" by his students, he used to teach illiterate inmates at the court jail as a volunteer; he also brought cigarettes and distributed them to the prisoners there. One time he came to me and, handing me a piece of paper, said: "Tadeusz, what are those rascals playing at? It's not enough that they've pilfered cigarettes from my pockets, cigarettes which I'd intended to give them anyway, now they're poking fun at me." I read the piece of paper: "Dear Professor, thanks for the smokes. Please bring vodka next time and we'll learn better."

From time to time I would meet Professor Wroński's son, Dr Józef Wroński, a friend of mine who organised clandestine secondary school classes in Podgórze (a proletarian district) because, as we know, the Germans had closed down all the secondary schools across the entire area of the General Government.

In the pharmacy I worked alongside three qualified ladies: Irena Droździkowska, Helena Krywaniuk and Aurelia Danek-Czortowa. From the very beginning of the ghetto's foundation, they all joined the effort to bring aid to the people imprisoned inside it. As long as the Jews could leave the ghetto with a ghetto pass, they could deal with many of their own personal affairs. But when the ghetto was closed and leaving was no longer possible, these three women began to play a distinct role. They carried out requests, delivered mail, and mediated in various matters between ghetto residents and Poles living outside it. They did food shopping for people, bought gifts required by the Jews for various purposes, and tried to get medicines which were difficult to obtain (and which were often smuggled from the Reich). They brought in various little items which the Jews had entrusted to their Polish friends when they were forced to leave their home district and move into the ghetto. Not knowing what conditions in the closed ghetto would be like, or whether or not they would be subject to searches, many Jews had left money and valuable objects with Polish friends for safekeeping. As it later turned out, many managed to survive hard times both in the ghetto and at Płaszów concentration camp — and even at camps further afield — thanks to deliveries of money and other trinkets they had safely deposited beyond the ghetto walls. One person who acted as a go-between was Dr Michał Weichert, who became the head of the JUS (Jewish Social Aid organisation) and who had access to a number of smaller camps outside the ghetto and Płaszów.

Everyone knew that helping the Jews, delivering smuggled notes, letters or valuable items, was a dangerous business.

I can say without the slightest exaggeration that we were well-liked by everyone and that throughout the entire existence of the ghetto we never had a single altercation, disagreeable squabble or unpleasant experience with any of the ghetto inhabitants. At every step of the way we met with extreme gratitude, which was perhaps not even entirely justified. The dozens of letters we received from the camps and, after their liberation, from countries all over Europe are proof of the enduring nature of the friendships forged during our time together in the ghetto.

In the first few weeks of the ghetto's existence, the pharmacy was sometimes closed on Sundays (the directive ordering the pharmacy to be open day and night, including holidays and Sundays, was issued eight months after the ghetto was established). This allowed the ghetto residents to apply for a pass to leave the ghetto to go to another pharmacy. In the initial period they were also permitted to leave the ghetto if we stamped and wrote a note on the prescription stating that we didn't have a given medicine in stock. We did this for anyone who asked.

On those Sundays off, I would sometimes go with friends to a café on Limanowski Street which was famous in the ghetto for its exquisite whole bean coffee and delicious home-made cakes. There was a great restaurant on Lwowska Street, right next to the entrance gate, serving *ferfel* with black pudding, Jewish-style fish and, on Saturdays, *cholent* — a traditional Jewish stew and a ghetto speciality. On warm, sunny days, people would spend their free time in the square on Józefińska Street (next to the OD building) or on the hill at Krzemionki (a tiny section of which lay inside the ghetto walls). There they took in the fresh air, surrendering themselves to an illusion of freedom, if only for a short while.

At this time the ghetto was rocked by some sensational news. We found out that the eminent Krakow ophthalmologist, Dr Edmund Rosenhauch, had been brought here one evening. He was living in a flat on Zgoda Square. He was being kept under house arrest and OD guards were posted to ensure he didn't go anywhere. It was said that SS General Krüger was going to be his private patient. However, the anticipated consultation did not take place — Dr Rosenhauch mysteriously disappeared from the ghetto. It later transpired that he had gone to Warsaw and survived the occupation there by dressing up as a monk and hiding in one of the capital's monasteries. Rosenhauch's escape to Warsaw was also believed to be the work of Aleksander Förster.

In the autumn of 1941, the administrative district of Krakow was enlarged to incorporate surrounding districts. As a result, the Jews living in those areas were forced to move into the Krakow ghetto immediately. I can still recall that Yom Kippur — one of the most important Jewish holidays — was designated as the last day for the move. The Germans' predilection for spitefulness knew no limits. That day it was exceptionally cold and rainy in the evening. Dozens of people, many with small children, stood in the freezing cold, buried under stacks of parcels and pots and pans, waiting to be admitted to a ghetto which was already bursting at the seams; the population was an estimated seventeen thousand people.

Life went by here in a strange way. From the early hours of the morning, people gathered at the entrance gate, getting ready to go outside. The unemployed, the sick and the elderly stayed behind in the ghetto. In the evening, the ghetto would fill up again, and people stood around or walked in groups, chatting, telling stories, commenting on the latest news from the front, or shopping; the restaurants and bakeries were full, and street traders did great business selling cigarettes, biscuits and sandwiches.

And that is what it was like every day — each day was similar to the next. People started to get used to the new conditions, and even began to believe it would be possible to survive like this, provided things stayed the same, as long as it didn't get any worse. Weeks and months went by…

One day the Germans gave an order for about one thousand people to be removed from the ghetto, because of its overpopulation problem. The old and the unemployed would be the first to go. The Judenrat, in cooperation with the OD, would have to carry out this operation.

This was the first major task to fall upon Symche Spira. Blindly devoted to the Germans, this man carried out every order and every instruction with the greatest precision; he would guess at and anticipate their thoughts, outdo them in zeal and impress them by not thinking about or questioning anything. The order meant everything to him, he cared about nothing else. Symche Spira was a megalomaniac and a daydreamer, a textbook psychopath, a neurasthenic, an embittered person who frequently suffered from gallstones. He was a sex maniac who was always looking for new, uncomplicated love affairs, and a semi-literate who spoke Polish and German equally badly. An egocentric, mechanical human being, this mindless robot carried out the Gestapo's orders as if he were hypnotised. He had a private secretary, who also happened to be one of his girlfriends.

Spira got down to work on the Germans' command. News of the order spread through the ghetto like wildfire until it had reached every last household. The inhabitants were seized with terror, gripped by universal anxiety. The OD compiled lists of names, and those who found themselves on these lists were dragged from their houses, from their beds, in the middle of the night and taken to the police station. The following day their papers were inspected to check who worked where; if it transpired that a person was not employed anywhere, he or she was detained and put in the OD courtyard. The German order said that these people would be deported to other localities. Not everybody believed this. At the pharmacy we spent a fearful and uncertain night with a small group of friends who preferred to be away from their own homes — because no one knew whether there would be more arrests that night too.

It was a strange night; hardly anybody got a wink of sleep. At dawn people quietly began to leave the pharmacy through the back door via the annexe courtyard, each going their separate ways, leaving at intervals. Danger lurked down every alley, and any loud conversation at such an early hour, any small group of people seen walking together aroused interest.

The following day, at around ten o'clock in the morning, the streets of the ghetto were a strange sight to behold. Groups of people stood on street corners, commenting on the order and discussing what would happen next. Their eyes were fixed on the OD building, the starting point for a parade of people walking into the unknown.

And they came... The news spread further through the crowd. People came out of their tenements or opened their windows — everyone in the ghetto watched what was happening in the streets. The motionless, half-demented gaze of the crowd was fixed blankly on the procession of deportees. The procession — old people, men, women and children — came down Targowa Street and across Zgoda Square towards Płaszów. On their backs they carried their most valuable possessions and whatever they considered to be the most useful objects for their journey into an unknown future. The OD men marched alongside them. A strange silence prevailed. Nobody was shouting at anybody, nobody was beating anybody. Like a funeral cortege, the people made their way towards the entrance gate. As they passed by, they could see the pain-stricken, terrified expressions on the faces of their closest friends and relatives. They went out of the ghetto, leaving behind them the tears of those who remained, the pain of saying goodbye, and the illusory hope that they would see one another again.

At the station in Płaszów, the deportees were loaded into freight wagons and given bread for the journey (which had been baked throughout the night in ghetto bakeries at the district's expense). The train set off and took them to the Lublin region, a few hundred kilometres away from Krakow. It stopped at a designated place, the wagon doors were opened and those inside were forced to get out. They were then ordered to split up and go to nearby settlements. The dumbstruck deportees had only one desire: to return to the ghetto as quickly as possible, to their own people, so they could be together again; but the Germans threatened to kill anyone who returned to Krakow.

Some of them did make it back to the ghetto after several days, others after several weeks. They came by any means possible. Some had come by train, after removing their arm bands and thus risking harsh penalties for contravening the Nazis' orders; others had come on carts, in private cars, and even military vehicles. The rest of them made their way back on foot.

From time to time people in the ghetto died after ending up on a list compiled by Jewish agent to the Gestapo, Szymon Szpic, in collusion with OD Kommandant Spira. Suspects were usually dragged from their homes in the middle of the night, taken to the OD building and transported early the next morning in heavily guarded German cars either to Pomorska Street or to some unknown location where they would disappear without trace. There were many such cases. Jews were killed and, in the early days, so were the few Poles who ran businesses in the ghetto. Apparently, my name once ended up on one of these lists. However, before the list was issued, news of its existence reached the ears of my physician friend, Dr Blau. As a result of her efforts, and those of other friends of mine, Szpic, the man who drew up the list, was persuaded to remove my name. The accusation Szpic was going to charge me with had to do with the large number of ghetto residents who kept gathering at the pharmacy during the night. The charming Dr Blau told me this several months later.

Dr Blau's intervention saved my life that time. Dr Blau had a younger brother in the ghetto, Carlos, who vaguely remembered me from the pharmacy. After the loss of his parents and the murder of his sister (Dr Blau), he ended up in a German camp. He was freed when the war ended. After a lifetime of struggle, he left Poland, then Europe, and finally settled in faraway Costa Rica. He is now a successful industrialist, a rich man, married to a charming and extremely striking Spanish woman. They have several children and are very happy. He sought out my address and wrote me a long, heartfelt letter. He introduced himself and reminisced about Krakow, the house where he was born, and the streets where he used to play. His parents often told him about us and our pharmacy. Even though he had left Poland so many years ago, his written and spoken Polish was faultless.

He has visited Krakow twice with his wife — they liked everything and were thoroughly delighted by the city. I spent some unforgettable times with them. They told me, and keep writing to say that even though they have no relatives or close friends left in Krakow, they come to see me. How moving it is to hear such words after so many years. We still keep in touch, and look forward to seeing each other again.

I had a similar experience in 1959 when I received a letter from Hirsch Pariser, who also knew me by sight. He was the son of a very rich man, who with a relative was the joint owner of some enormous warehouses containing flour, buckwheat, rice and other agricultural produce. These warehouses were situated on the banks of the Vistula river. The company was called "Dränger-Pariser, Agricultural Stores". Hirsch Pariser was in the ghetto as a very young man. After losing his parents he was transported from the ghetto to a German camp. Then came the end of the war and long-desired freedom. The young Hirsch settled for good in Belgium, married and had two sons. In his first letter, he described his tragic experiences in the ghetto, the death of his beloved parents and relatives, his miserable existence in the German camps and his rescue at the eleventh hour. He warmly invited me to visit him in Belgium: "Do come, my wife and I would be very pleased to see you". I went there and spent an entire month at the Parisers' charming home. In the evenings we would remember the events of yesteryear. My visit to the Parisers was a very moving experience. I shall always be grateful to my hosts for their great kindness and friendship.

I have had many similar cases — young people looking for my address years after the war had ended, so they could send me a few kind words…

Just who was this Szpic who put my name on the arrest list? He was a shrivelled man of about fifty-five. Tall and slim, he had olive skin, a slight stoop and a permanent sneer. Szpic became known on the streets of Krakow before the war when he went on trial for fraud and obtaining money under false pretences (in exchange for securing non-existent jobs). He was sentenced to several years in prison for his crimes. He was the terror of the ghetto, and woe betide anyone who crossed him — that poor wretch's days were well and truly numbered. Szpic died at the hands of the Gestapo, as did everyone who was in their service. He and a man known as Whitebeard — a fellow spy in the pay of the Gestapo — were sent to the Radom area to conduct an alleged hunt for saboteurs operating there. Some time later we received news that both had died, and this was confirmed by the Germans. That was when it became clear how the Nazis paid these servile traitors for their work.

Many young people were arrested as a result of lists like those, including the aforementioned Maryla Schenkerówna. A German came for her in person. On entering her parents' flat on Józefińska Street, he asked her mother: "*Wo ist diese schöne Blonde*?"

When Schenkerówna appeared, the German looked at her for a long time, then said: "*Ach, du bist diese Schöne... nun gut, komm mit.*"

She went to the OD and was then transported to Auschwitz, where she died of pneumonia. I remember

11. Helena Krywaniuk

how much effort and how much money her father spent trying to save her. One German took it upon himself to intervene, and he even sought out an SS man who, for a set amount, was supposed to facilitate her escape and take her to Holland, where she had close relatives. The SS man received some of the money upfront; he was to get the rest only once the relatives had confirmed Maryla's safe arrival in writing. A while later, this SS man brought a letter written in Schenkerówna's hand. She wrote that she was in Holland and that she was healthy and happy. However, a few weeks later, a letter arrived from her relatives in which there was no mention of Maryla. The German's deception came to light, especially when a card arrived from Auschwitz a few days later, on which their daughter had written: "I am healthy and doing well!"

As well as Szpic, it is worth mentioning some other informers working both inside and outside the ghetto, to whom the Germans had entrusted a wide variety of functions. These include: Julek Appel (aka Whitebeard), Stefania Brandtstätterówna (alias Poklewska), Chilowicz and his wife, Finkelstein, Förster, the aforementioned Marcel Grüner, Marcel Goldberg, Kleinberger, Kerner, Michał Pacanower, Szymon Rosen, Marian Rotkopf, Ignacy Taubmann, Weininger, and Weismann. There were many others for whom we didn't have one hundred percent proof. Informers could be found in every workplace and institution in the ghetto. One such place was the *Zollfahndungsstelle*, where the informants Brodman

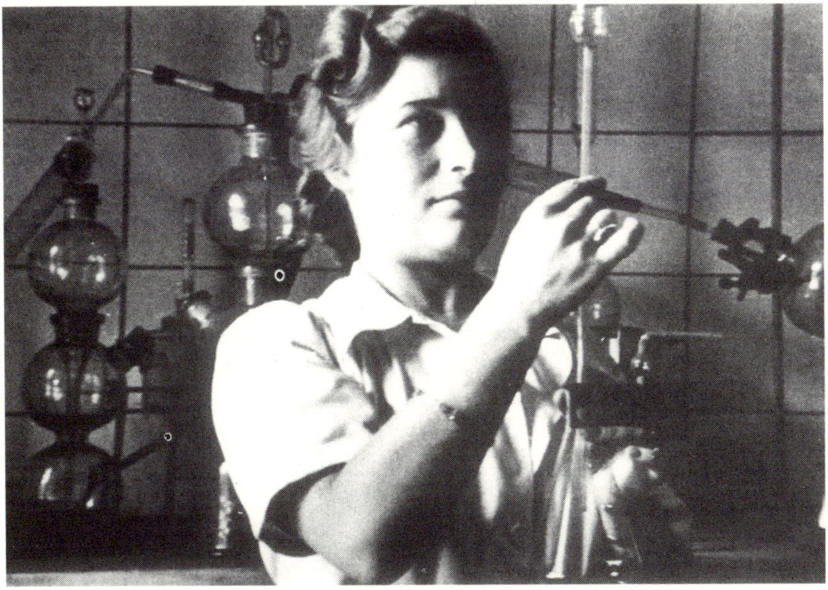

12. Irena Droździkowska

and Steinfeld provided many services to the Germans. We had the names of informers written down on prescriptions, and I kept these throughout the period of the occupation. Nearly all of them died at the hands of the Gestapo or the Polish underground.

There was an extremely dangerous married couple in the service of the Gestapo, called the Selingers. He was of medium height, well-dressed with neatly-combed dark hair; she was a short peroxide blonde, with a doll-like appearance and a poor command of Polish. They collaborated with SS-Obersturmführer Theodor Heinemayer, the Gestapo's political affairs officer. She used to eavesdrop on the Germans' conversations in the café; he was willing to carry out any duties the Gestapo assigned him. He informed on Jews using Aryan identity documents, and he reported Poles who had contact with Jews.

The Selingers' end casts a ray of light on the cynicism of the Germans. Realising that sooner or later he would end up dead like all the other informers, Selinger decided to test the water in Hungary, to where everyone hoping to survive most often fled. He first crossed the border on his own and then returned for his wife a week later. And that was when he was summoned by Theodor Heinemayer, who knew everything.

"If you want to run away, don't be foolish and don't take risks because they'll catch you at the border and then you'll be done for. If you want I'll give you a letter for the chief of police in Nowy Targ, which should facilitate your escape. It's quite simple, I can help you. You've done a lot for me, and I'll prove to you that Germans are decent people."

Selinger didn't know how to thank him. Heinemayer wrote the letter and gave it to him. A few days later the Selingers travelled to Nowy Targ. There they reported to the chief of police and handed over the letter of recommendation. The German took the letter and asked them to take a seat — after all, this was a letter from not just anyone, but from Heinemayer himself. After reading it, the police chief told the couple to follow him to the courtyard; there he read out the contents of the letter, in which Heinemayer ordered that those who delivered it should be shot. Heinemayer's order was carried out. It later transpired that only Mrs Selinger died; her husband lived to see the end of the war. How he did this is unknown. He showed up in Krakow after the war, but apparently later moved to America.

I heard this story from the deputy Schupo Kommandant Bousko, who in turn had heard it at a Gestapo party, where Heinemayer bragged to fellow guests about wanting to test how smart Selinger was. If he were cunning, he would open the letter, read it and run for it. If he didn't open it, he'd deserve his fate. According to another version of the story, Selinger learned of the letter's contents and fled to Hungary with his wife.

I appeared as a witness at Heinemayer's trial in Hanover in 1978. I sat face to face with the defendant, who had been on release pending trial. The kindly-looking fat old man before me looked nothing like the beastly Heinemayer from the days of the ghetto. He sat motionless through four hours of witness testimony, as if under a spell, staring straight ahead. He was acquitted.

Despite the ostensible calm, the mood in the ghetto was deteriorating. The Judenrat's endless meetings with the German authorities regarding the overpopulation of the ghetto, the size of which would have to be reduced, filled everyone with anxiety. And even though the word "deportation" was not mentioned explicitly, people began to work out that there was something nasty in the air. The uncertainty wore them out and took away their peace.

Their speculation and premonitions turned out to be well-founded. In June 1942, the ghetto was surrounded at night by a cordon of Sonderdienst officers. Police guards and barbed wire had been put around the walls. Nobody on the outside could get near the boundaries of the ghetto. Jews whose homes faced onto the Aryan district were not allowed to open or appear in the windows or to go out onto their balconies. The punishment for disobedience was a bullet — the Germans would shoot at the windows if they saw someone standing at them.

Panic arose in the ghetto. The time limits set for deportation became the topic of every conversation, who would go and who would stay. Nobody could say anything for certain. The Germans did not disclose any of their plans and nobody dared ask them. Besides, anything they said would have been a lie.

From 29 to 31 May 1942, committees comprised of Gestapo officers and Arbeitsamt personnel worked in the JUS building. Tables were set up in the main hall of the former savings bank; at each one sat a Gestapo officer and a clerk from the employment office. And in front of each table people stood in long queues as they tremulously waited to learn of their fate. Outside crowds of people huddled for hours in lines several hundred metres long. The Gestapo decided on the spot who would stay and who would leave the ghetto. Those who fell into the latter group asked fearfully: "Where are they taking us?" "What are they going to do with us?" "Will they let us take any of our things?". They tried their best to reassure one another. Nobody believed mass extermination would happen; at that point nobody could have dreamt of crematoria, toxic gas and piles of burning bodies. For the first time rumours began to spread that the Germans were secretly saying the deportees were going to Ukraine to do agricultural work at open labour camps. The German railwaymen were talking about some enormous barracks that stood there waiting for the transports to arrive, and about the life being set up in this newly built barrack town, with restaurants, reading rooms and cinemas available for everyone. They said that the Jews would be paid for their work, that there they would be sure to survive the war in peace and quiet. People began to believe them. A new worry arose: what about food? Would they be allowed to take large quantities of provisions with them? And still people kept trying in every way possible to obtain an *SS und Polizeiführer* stamp on their Kennkarten — this was the stamp that gave you the right to stay in the ghetto. At the time, no one imagined that this stamp decided who lived and who died. And whether or not you got it was entirely at the whim of a German; neither proof that you had a job nor what type of occupation you had were deciding factors. There were many paradoxical stories: someone could be refused a stamp, only to return to the very same table an hour later and get one with no trouble at all. Somebody else might be refused a stamp at one table, but get it at the next. Coincidence, luck, the mood and whims of the Gestapo officer, how many friends you had in high places, how much money you had, the purity and size of the diamond you offered — all these were possible factors in deciding whether you stayed in the ghetto or were deported. The registration was over in two days. People without a stamp awaited their fate.

On 1 June 1942, the OD received the order to take all those without stamps from their homes and escort them to Zgoda Square. During the night, the OD conducted door to door inspections of Kennkarten. Those marked down for deportation were detained. The same thing happened in the early hours of the following day, i.e. on the morning of 2 June 1942. Once again, the pharmacy was full of friends during the night.

As dawn broke on 2 June, a procession of men and women moved forward — it was a ghastly, nightmarish scene. Most of them were elderly, but there were quite a few young people too. Frantic parents looked on as their children were led away.

Like shadows, like apparitions from a ghost story, they slowly trailed along, carrying on their shoulders possessions as heavy as the tragedy of their fate.

Zgoda Square slowly began to fill up with people and piles of packages, suitcases and luggage of every kind imaginable. The sun beat down more and more fiercely, heralding a major heat wave. Throats were parched from thirst, nerves frayed to the extreme and eyes filled with fear, terror and madness.

Two cars drove through the entrance gate from Zgoda Square and stopped about fifty metres from my pharmacy. Two Gestapo officers got out of the first car, one of whom approached those sitting in the second. They exchanged a few words and then the second car drove off in the direction of the OD building.

I opened the pharmacy as usual that day. I stood inside and watched to see what would happen. What was actually going on? After a while I saw the two Gestapo officers who had stayed in Zgoda Square pull their revolvers from their holsters and slowly move towards the pharmacy. We could hear the clatter of their boots from the now totally silent square. I couldn't understand a thing — I gave my colleagues a surprised look and we exchanged a few remarks about what was happening before our very eyes. We couldn't understand what they wanted, or who they had come for. This was really very odd. Just then the door opened and both

Germans came in. They were tall, handsome, dressed in splendid Sonderdienst uniforms, wearing caps with matt death's head insignia on them. They walked up to the counter without a word of greeting. I asked them: "Wünschen?" — but received no reply. Their steely, penetrating gazes roamed over our faces, slowly moving to the pharmacy equipment and the medicines. It touched every object in the room, slid onto the walls, stopped briefly on a holy picture, and a burning lamp, and then came back to me and my staff... A deathly silence filled the room. A moment later, without uttering a word, they put their revolvers down on the marble counter, took out cartridge clips and loaded their weapons. A dull click rang out each time they loaded a new cartridge, and then they did it again. A faint smile flickered across their lips and then, again without a word of farewell, they left the pharmacy. I found the entire episode totally inexplicable.

The streets leading to Zgoda Square began to empty. People hid in doorways. Spira and his personal staff were running around like crazy. The Gestapo officers left the pharmacy, closing the door behind them. We watched as one of them slowly aimed his revolver in the direction of Józefińska Street. The OD men called out to each other. Then he fired...once...twice...three times. And slowly he lowered his smoking revolver. The voices died away; all we could hear through the deathly silence were the rapid footsteps of the OD men as they ran past. Why had he fired? Who was he aiming at? Did he hit anyone? Was it just a warning? All these thoughts and questions whizzed through our minds. As it turned out, someone *was* injured, but fortunately not fatally. The first Gestapo officer who had fired into the ghetto was SS-Sturmscharführer and Kriminalsekretär Wilhelm Kunde, a Jewish Affairs officer in the Sicherheitspolizei. The first person injured was Dr Weichert, the chairman of the JUS, the Jewish Social Aid organisation. The bullet had ricocheted and hit him in the arm.

More cars carrying Gestapo officers entered the ghetto. We saw a wide variety of uniforms and insignia. There were representatives of a number of police and military units, clerks from various departments of the Stadthauptmann — all of them had come to feast their eyes on the extraordinary spectacle.

More and more groups of Jews entered Zgoda Square. Slowly, the tightly packed crowd began to fill the empty space. At first people stood, then after a while they sat down on the ground or on their packs. The sun was beating down mercilessly, parching their throats. Opposite the pharmacy, by the wall of a tenement building, stood a team of doctors in white coats, nurses, hospital matrons and stretcher-bearers. The white of their medical gowns stood out incredibly strangely against the black and grey of the crowd waiting to be deported. The pharmacy door kept opening as the doctors, matrons and OD men took drugs to give to the deportees; valerian, bromide — sedatives and heart medication were our last gifts to them. Some sitting, some standing, the crowd waited, frozen by fear and uncertainty.

13. Aurelia Danek-Czortowa

Trolleys and wagons arrived in the square. The deportees started running towards them, pushing to find a seat and somewhere to put their baggage. In the crush, pushing and shoving, strength and age determined who got there first. In the space of a few minutes, all the wagons were literally stuffed with people and luggage. The SS men observed all this with derisive smiles on their faces. For the second time that day, the pharmacy door was pushed open by the Gestapo. Two young officers entered; they must have been in their mid-twenties. This time they managed to let out a "Guten Tag". They asked who owned the pharmacy, and how they could get to the balcony on the floor above. I told them. They thanked me and left. They took photographs from the balcony, so they could show the world how humanely the German nation was treating the people being deported — or "resettled", as they put it, because you weren't allowed to use the word *Aussiedlung*. In similar fashion, you couldn't say "ghetto" — it was the "Jewish district".

We heard the click of photos being taken, and the sound of the film being wound on in their steel reporter's Leicas... and they were finished... they had all the deceitful propaganda photos they needed. They could now be sent out into the world, perhaps they'd become historical records one day. And still the people waited. The heat was unrelenting, people were fainting and collapsing from exhaustion. Then came a curt order: "*Alle heraus! Schnell — raus!*" How terrible that shrieking sounded in our ears. And in the blink of an eye, they began emptying the carts. The Germans, and the OD men at their command, started throwing out bags and suitcases, dragging out the elderly sitting inside, and shoving the younger ones as quickly as possible. People looked at one another in terror — what was going on? Was that entire farce with the carts staged just so they could take their propaganda photos?

On hearing the terrifying screams of the Germans, the crowd got to its feet, then sat down, then got back up again. The bodies were packed together even more tightly. The crowd began to leave Zgoda Square; slowly at first, then more quickly and then at a run, all the while being shoved, beaten and goaded by the Germans' inarticulate yelling. The luggage was dreadfully heavy. Some people abandoned the heaviest items, others had these items taken from them by SS men. The crowd of deportees speedily snaked its way along the tram lines to Płaszów. Their oppressors screamed louder and louder: "*Raus, raus, los, schnell!*" These words hounded people for the entire duration of the occupation — you could hear them everywhere, all the time. Exhausted and bloodied, the deportees fell to the ground, picked themselves back up and fell down again, their packs slipping from their bleeding hands. Some of them didn't pick them up again — why should they drag them along on a journey leading to death? An hour or so later the square was empty. Carts loaded with bread continued to arrive — the last gift the deportees received from those left behind (on orders from the Judenrat, bread

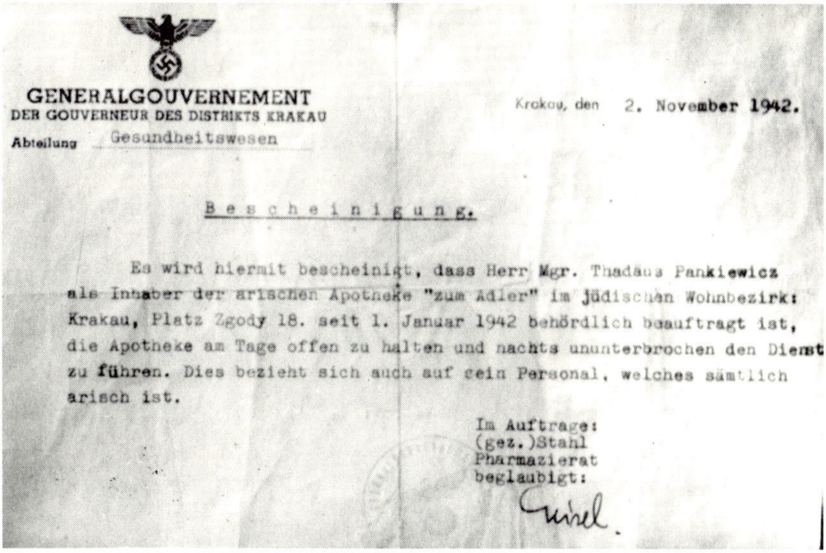

GENERALGOUVERNEMENT
DER GOUVERNEUR DES DISTRIKTS KRAKAU
Abteilung Gesundheitswesen

Krakau, den 2. November 1942.

Bescheinigung.

Es wird hiermit bescheinigt, dass Herr Mgr. Thadäus Pankiewicz als Inhaber der arischen Apotheke "zum Adler" im jüdischen Wohnbezirk: Krakau, Platz Zgody 18. seit 1. Januar 1942 behördlich beauftragt ist, die Apotheke am Tage offen zu halten und nachts ununterbrochen den Dienst zu führen. Dies bezieht sich auch auf sein Personal, welches sämtlich arisch ist.

Im Auftrage:
(gez.)Stahl
Pharmazierat
beglaubigt:

14. Certificate permitting Tadeusz Pankiewicz
and his colleagues to operate
a twenty-four-hour pharmacy in the ghetto district

was baked the night before in all the bakeries in the ghetto). The square was now empty and silent — all that was left in the previously packed space were discarded bundles and luggage, and liturgical books wrapped in velvet were dotted around here and there. Those who remained couldn't believe it had all really happened. The tremendous shock and terror had removed their ability to comprehend the facts objectively.

German dignitaries, high-ranking SS men and Gestapo officers followed the deportees in their cars. Those responsible for Jewish affairs stayed behind at the OD building, and even they left the ghetto two hours later. But the walls remained heavily guarded: a visible sign that the day's operation wasn't over yet.

That night was a terrible and exhausting one, when nobody got a wink of sleep. For those who were left, the uncertainty about what tomorrow would bring and the feeling of powerlessness against such brutality left them mentally shattered. A whole host of friends came to the pharmacy that night. They kept looking at the clock on the wall; its hands seemed not to be moving. Nobody fell asleep, everybody was waiting.

Some of the people who were refused a stamp or who had given up trying (entrusting their fate to destiny instead), had not reported for the first deportation and were now trying to change the Germans' decision by any means possible. A continuous stream of telephone calls were made from the ghetto to officials at all sorts of workplaces where Jews were employed. In many cases these interventions had the desired effect. The officials would either come to the ghetto in person, or sort the matter out by speaking to the ghetto's Arbeitsamt, and even Gestapo officers if necessary.

The Germans were unsatisfied with the number of deportees. According to their figures, many people without stamps had failed to turn up.

An order was issued requiring all residents to present their documents for inspection, and anyone without permission to stay in the ghetto was to be detained. On the night of 3–4 June 1942, the Gestapo, Sonderdienst and OD men inspected people's documents, stopping them to check their identification papers in the streets, entering hospitals and nursing homes, and searching tenement buildings and flats from top to bottom — all this accompanied by punching, kicking and shoving. This operation lasted until the morning of 4 June when, at dawn, heavily armed Sonderdienst units entered the ghetto, ready for combat. For the first time, Polish police units (i.e. the Blue Police), and Polish youths who had been forced into entering the so-called Baudienst, joined the German police. The German police took up positions along the buildings on Zgoda Square. In front of them were racks of rifles; behind them, just in front of the pharmacy window, stood the Baudienst. The Blue Police were standing opposite, and next to them, in a tiny side street, stood Jewish doctors, nurses and orderlies with stretchers. Members of the medical service had managed to get the appropriate stamps on their passes without any trouble at all. But for how long? The little group comprised ten people. Their job — the result of a German order — was allegedly to assist anyone if they fainted.

And so the procession of deportees began. The first lot of people were driven out onto Zgoda Square; kicked and punched, they moved like shadows, at a slow, solemn and dignified pace. Others came running in small groups or on their own, and yet others looked as if they had gone mad. All around them were German police guards with rifles in their hands, their fingers on the triggers, ready to shoot. The crowd was passing in front of my windows. All of this was accompanied by persistent screaming, relentless beating, kicking and shooting. Many were killed, many were injured — and the deportation had only just begun.

Unfolding before my very eyes, as if in some horrific kaleidoscope, were scenes not of this world. The ghetto boomed with gunfire. The soldiers carried rifles, the SS officers had revolvers, pokers, sticks and canes. The hospital orderlies had to dodge the firing and squeeze through the crowd to remove the dead and the injured. The Germans were firing like madmen, at anyone at all, anyone they felt like. The sight of blood evidently aroused their savagery and sadism.

During the first deportation, people were still allowed to take luggage with them (in accordance with an official German order), and it was not searched on Zgoda Square. This time, however, the Germans subjected many people to detailed searches, of their luggage and their person, either in front of everyone on Zgoda Square, or in doorways and shops. As a general rule, the luggage was taken from its owner, and the searches were accompanied by beatings, regardless of age or gender.

During this deportation, I remember how a young and pretty woman came hurrying into the pharmacy. She had been driven out with the crowd onto Zgoda Square (from where almost all of the transports left). She pushed past some people standing inside, ran through the other rooms in the pharmacy and disappeared from sight. Meanwhile, other bizarre things were happening at the pharmacy: now and then somebody would come in to give us pieces of paper with their last requests or changed decisions written on them, asking us to pass them onto their loved ones. People who had been hit and injured asked us for help. In 1956, I received a letter from Israel, written by the same young woman. She reminded me of the events of that day: taking advantage of the confusion, she hid under one of the tables in another room in the pharmacy and waited for some time, until she could get out of the back door, across the courtyard, and then through the gate which led into another street. Her name was Irena Halpern and she came from a well-off business family. Her father owned a fur company on Grodzka Street in Krakow. Her parents were killed during the October deportations of 1942. She had been sent to the concentration camp in Płaszów, and then transferred to another camp in Skarżysko. She finally ended up in a camp in Częstochowa, where she held out until the end of the war. After the camp was liberated, she made her way to Israel, via Germany. Irena and her husband were extremely hospitable when I stayed with them during my trip to Israel.

Every now and then doctors, nurses and OD men would come running into the pharmacy to pick up medicines and dressings for people who had been battered or wounded, or had fainted. I humbly beg to mention that we distributed tranquillisers, sleeping pills, painkillers and dressings free of charge: we didn't take a penny from those headed for certain death. The seriously wounded were taken to the hospital on Józefińska Street.

More and more people poured into the square, after being dragged from their hiding places. Old people, women and children drifted like ghosts in front of the pharmacy windows. I saw an old woman of about seventy, with ruffled grey hair, striding along a few feet away from a larger group of deportees. She walked slowly and calmly and her glazed eyes, wide with fear, stared straight ahead. She wore only a dress and a pair of slippers, and she wasn't carrying any luggage, not even a handbag. In both arms she was hugging something small and black to her ageing breast. It was a tiny dog, a miniature pinscher; she had taken the dearest thing she had left, the only thing she refused to part with.

A young girl of around fourteen walked past, laughing and randomly waving her arms about. She was mentally ill and well known to everyone in the ghetto. She walked barefoot and wore a tattered nightdress. The sight of that girl laughing and smiling made us shiver, when all around her people were collapsing and quaking with terror. Old and young people passed by, some were clothed, others wore only the underwear they were found in when dragged from their beds. There were patients and people recovering from major surgery and lengthy illnesses. Driven by fear, beaten and bloodied, they rushed past the jeering soldiers.

A seventy-year-old blind man, also well known to many in the ghetto, came out of a building on Zgoda Square. Dark glasses covered his sightless eyes. He had lost his eyesight fighting the Germans in 1914 at the Italian front. On his left arm he wore a yellow band with three black circles on it, which denoted blindness. He walked with his head held high, led by his son on one side and his wife on the other. "He's lucky he can't see, it will be easier for him to die," one of the nurses said to us. On his breast he had pinned a medal he had won in the war — perhaps the Germans would take this into consideration? At the beginning people initially reasoned in these terms.

Behind the blind man came an old one-legged man on crutches. The Germans approached them. One of them ran up to the blind man at a slow, dance-like pace and shrieked appallingly: "Schnell!" This encouraged others to start amusing themselves. Two SS men went up to the old man with one leg and shouted at him to hurry up and run; another came up behind him and began hitting his crutches with the butt of his rifle, causing him to fall to the ground. The German screamed like a madman, threatening to shoot him. All of this took place just behind the blind man, who saw nothing and heard only the Germans' inhuman screams and the wails of the injured, interspersed with cascades of laughter. A German soldier went up to the crippled man lying on the ground and helped him to his feet, while a German officer eagerly took photographs for their records of "German assistance during the humanitarian resettlement of the Jews". For a moment we thought that there might perhaps be just one human being among these torturers who couldn't stand the bullying of defenceless and innocent people in the final hours of their lives. Unfortunately, there was no such person in the history of the Krakow ghetto.

As they had had their fill of the maltreated one-legged cripple, they decided to try the same on the blind war veteran. First they chased away his son, and then his wife, then they kept tripping him up, enjoying the sight of him falling to the ground. This time they didn't help him up, he had to do it on his own, egged on by the terrifying screams of the SS men standing over him. This entertainment was repeated several times. This cruelty was a truly shocking sight. Nobody knew what amused them more, the physical pain inflicted on him every time he fell to the ground, or the despair experienced by his wife and son standing nearby, silent and powerless against the violence.

It is difficult to detail each separate incident, every variety of German crime, every lawless act that took place right in front of our eyes. The details of each separate case appeared quite similar — they all began with beating and often ended in shooting. In reality, however, they all looked entirely different. Each had its own tragic significance.

Gunfire rang out across the ghetto, people fell down dead or injured; each German crime left in its wake a trail of blood on the streets and pavements. There were more and more people in the square. The heat, as in previous days, was incredible. There was no water to be had, and even if there had been, we still wouldn't have been allowed to distribute it. Weak from the heat and thirst, people were fainting and falling to the ground. In front of the pharmacy stood a small military car and every now and then SS men would load it with briefcases full of valuables confiscated during the deportation raids. They took everything they laid their eyes on: rings, gold and metal watches, cigarette cases, even lighters. Some of the deportees watched the rest; others waited in the queue, with indifferent and apathetic expressions on their faces. They no longer cared about anything.

In the pharmacy we were finding out where people had been killed, who had committed suicide, where people were injured, and also the names of the victims. The hospitals were full to bursting, and the doctors were attending to the wounded and saving those who had tried to poison themselves. Many of those in danger of deportation owe their lives to Dr A. Biberstein, head of the hospital for infectious diseases on Rękawka Street.

Many people hid there, and Dr Biberstein gave them white aprons so they would look like hospital workers. He trusted that the Germans, for fear of infection, wouldn't enter the hospital. And he was right.

When would it all end? This question tormented everyone. I watched through the pharmacy window, standing far back so I couldn't be seen. The Gestapo didn't like their exterminations to be watched. The tram service was suspended during the deportations and even German cars weren't allowed to drive through the ghetto. I saw a group of high-ranking SS dignitaries approaching the pharmacy. They stopped right by the front door and I heard their voices — I could catch every word perfectly, especially as they were in the habit of barking instead of speaking. I moved quite close to the door and hid myself in a small recess in the wall. They were dissatisfied with the number of deportees and the assistance of the Judenrat. They unequivocally blamed its chairman, whose name came up now and then. A little later I heard one of the SS men shout, and then a whistle aimed at the OD men standing further down Targowa Street. I heard their footsteps as they came running. I saw that Spira was one of the people standing some distance from the SS men. He stood to attention and saluted as he was given a terse order to fetch immediately the chairman of the Judenrat, Dr Henryk Rosenzweig.

A thin man of about forty approached the group of Germans. He had a long, shrivelled face and made nervous gestures. He spoke to them relatively freely and

15. Sections of the wall behind the school
on Limanowski Street

his command of German was excellent. This man was called Dawid Gutter. A few minutes later, Rosenzweig appeared: he was an elderly gentleman with ruffled grey hair and no hat. He approached slowly, stopped in front of the Gestapo officers and SS men and gently bowed his head. There was a moment of silence and then the following terrible words fell from one of the SS men's mouth: "Rosenzweig, you are summarily dismissed from your post. This operation has not achieved satisfactory results, both in terms of numbers and in the logistics of getting people to the square. And you are to blame!" As he said this, he struck Rosenzweig on the head. I watched in horror from only two metres away... Dr Rosenzweig didn't utter a word, but just gently bowed his head again and walked away. The Germans turned to Gutter and told him that from now on he was responsible for everything. "*Jawohl*," he replied and jumped to attention.

The ghetto had a new commissioner, for this was the title Gutter now held. Who was he? A former commercial traveller and magazine vendor, Gutter was an extremely nervous man — he moved very awkwardly — and he always seemed to be on the go. He was clever, zestful, energetic, and he equalled Spira in his ability to obey and execute German orders; he was, however, far more intelligent than Spira and more critical in his outlook. He had his own opinions and was able to slip sober thoughts into his eloquent speeches, and this was picked up on by many of his listeners. He let his promotion to such a "high-ranking" position by the Germans go to his

16. Sections of the ghetto wall
behind the school

head, and he soon developed a superiority complex, just as Spira had done. From the moment he was appointed, he threw himself into his work. During the deportation operations, he ran around like crazy from one lot of Germans to another, shouting and gesticulating wildly. As I watched him, I was in awe of his immense stamina.

Immediately after being stripped of his chairmanship, Dr Rosenzweig was arrested together with his entire family. He was added to the next group of deportees and sent to Bełżec extermination camp, where he died in the gas chamber. Doubtless the Germans saw him as a liability. He was a highly respectable, honest and intelligent man, a lawyer by education, someone who was able to think and reason. The title given to him by the Germans did not impress him; he undoubtedly saw it as a burden, as were all managerial positions at that time and in those circumstances for honourable people with a sense of dignity.

What was the general opinion of Dr Rosenzweig? He was accused of reacting too passively in situations where he could have brought some degree of relief without prejudicing the matter. For example, he could — some believed — have intervened to save doctors from deportation and have them taken off the transports.

Nobody really thought about the efficacy and appropriateness of such interventions. They accused the chairman of failing to take action, and at the same time of being too firm and lacking flexibility towards the differing views of his closest colleagues. This was interpreted as apathy, resignation and powerlessness in the face of violence, which had taken away his belief in the efficacy of any efforts whatsoever. He would gladly have resigned from his post, but he knew the dangers of doing so.

The deportation began. The square slowly started to empty. Some people left in vehicles, others went on foot, forced to move faster by screaming Germans. Shoved, kicked and punched, they ran along Lwowska Street and Wielicka Street — towards Płaszów. They were escorted along the way by Sonderdienst guards, who shot at anyone who couldn't keep up. Dead bodies lined the deportees' route, streams of blood flowed on the cobblestones.

At the train station in Płaszów, everyone was loaded into cattle trucks sprinkled with quicklime. The trucks had tiny barred windows at the top. Around a hundred and twenty people were crammed into each truck, then the doors were locked tight; each truck was heavily guarded by Germans. The deportees weren't allowed water or bread, and the heat was tremendous. The train began to move.

A few people had brought locksmith's tools with them and managed to save themselves from the transport by breaking the bars on the truck windows and jumping out while the train was moving; in doing so, they risked hitting railway poles, falling under the wheels of the speeding train and — most likely — a bullet from the policemen escorting the trucks.

There were also those who smashed out the floorboards while the train was in motion and then, when the train stopped at a station, slid to the ground below. The train set off and passed over people lying on the tracks. What happened to the escapees after that was down to luck.

A boy I knew later told me that he had jumped from a moving train, but he had been spotted. The German escorts fired a volley of shots and wounded him. He lost consciousness, rolled down an embankment and lay there for goodness knows how long. When he came to, it was dark and raining. He crawled for several hours before he came to the first cottage; he tramped from one house to the next for days on end. People didn't always open their doors to him, he didn't always hear kind words of sympathy, and they didn't always offer him something to eat. But nobody gave him up. He kept on walking for weeks and weeks. Time healed his wounds and he made it back to the ghetto, where he remained until 13 March 1943, when it was completely liquidated.

During the abovementioned deportation, I was visited again by one of the officers for Jewish Affairs, SS-Sturmscharführer Kunde. On the counter in my pharmacy he stamped Kennkarten for people recommended to him by Spira and Förster.

I recall the following scene involving Kunde which illustrates the sometimes downright inexplicable mentality of the Germans. Kunde was generally considered one of the most approachable Germans, as was his fellow officer for Jewish Affairs, SS-Sturmscharführer Heinrich; both men were known for the fact that they didn't beat people, didn't scream and were amenable to certain "arguments". As Kunde walked the streets of the ghetto, he was surrounded by people begging him to stamp their documents. He stood and chatted to them for quite a while, and the crowd got bigger and bigger. Suddenly he saw a German approaching on the other side of the street and, fearing he'd come under suspicion for talking to the Jews, he pulled out his revolver and began threatening to shoot. In fact, he did shoot: the bullet ricocheted off the ground and injured Dr Silberger. The crowd ran off in panic. One of those who fled was a young girl who couldn't have been more than twelve years old. Kunde chased after her, caught her and asked her why she had run away; he grabbed someone standing nearby to act as an interpreter. The terrified young girl stammered that she was afraid he'd shoot her.

"And what do you want from me?" he asked.

"A stamp for my mummy and daddy," she replied.

"Who are your parents?"

"My father is a cobbler."

Kunde told the child to bring Kennkarten for her entire family. He stamped them in the pharmacy. We made the most of the occasion to get these stamps for many others who just happened to be in the pharmacy at the time. The ladies were wonderful at taking advantage of Kunde's good mood. The lives of thousands of people lay in hands like these. The fates of thousands of human beings were often down to the whims of people like him.

The ghetto remained surrounded by the Sonderdienst. German police patrols roamed the streets at a steady pace. Now and then shots were fired from the guard posts around the ghetto, particularly those at Krzemionki, from where you could see the entire Jewish district as clear as daylight. And in the distance, on the other side of the Vistula, lay Krakow and the prominent mound of Wawel Castle, from whose tower flew the hated flag marked with a swastika.

CHAPTER III

LIEUTENANT BOUSKO — THE DEPORTATION OF 8 JUNE 1942 — THE DIMINISHING GHETTO — DIFFICULT LIVING CONDITIONS — THE DEPORTATION OF 28 OCTOBER 1942 — THE ATTITUDES OF THE PERSECUTED

During the June operation, a peculiar character showed up in the ghetto, a deputy commandant for the German police in Podgórze. His name was Lieutenant Oswald Bousko.

After sitting in the pharmacy for two days solid, I decided to get out of the ghetto, despite a warning from one of the older German policemen that I risked being shot. "These people," he said, looking around cautiously and gesturing towards some SS-men, "these people don't give a damn about anything. They don't care if you're an Aryan or whether you have a permit to be in the ghetto; in the ghetto they can do whatever they like and get away with it." I didn't listen to him and went out anyway. I made my way through the deserted streets and walked past the German police guard posts. The Germans looked at me with interest; as I wasn't wearing an armband, they clearly took me for a German, and I wasn't stopped until I reached the entrance gate. I passed through the gate and in front of me stood a tall German of around forty, with blond hair, hazel eyes, an oval face and a characteristic grimace at the corners of his mouth. He stared at me with a surprised look on his face. He bent low, put his hands behind his back and looked me in the eyes. He asked to see my papers and I gave them to him. He looked at them for a moment and handed them back to me. Then he began to rant. He didn't shout, he screamed. I couldn't understand what he wanted from me because he spoke in a Viennese dialect. In the end I realised what he was on about: I was leaving the ghetto without a German police escort. He said they could have shot me on the spot. I couldn't think why he cared so much about my life. I wondered and listened… He advised me to telephone the guard post at whichever exit I wanted to use in future, and said he'd send me a police escort. I was simply amazed at his concern, especially as he didn't know me.

Despite this German's terrifying screaming and ranting, I sensed in him a hint of fellow feeling (we can probably call it that) towards me as another human being. And in those days that meant a great deal. Just who was this policeman? His name was Bousko. In time I found out some interesting things about him. He was born in Vienna, the son of a low-ranking official, and when he was in his early teens he was shipped off to a monastery to become a monk. He ran away after a few months and set off on a trip around the world. He travelled across the whole of southern Europe on foot, and made it all the way to Turkey. After his travels he returned to Vienna and joined the police. He became a staunch member of the National Socialists, he regarded Hitler as God and was one of the first policemen in Austria to join the party.

He became a secret member of the SS while Dollfuss[1] was still in power office. After the annexation of Austria, he transformed himself into a resolute enemy of Hitler. He was the first to join him, and the first to leave him. He treated the Jewish population relatively kindly and his sympathy during every operation was genuine; he helped as much as he could, but he did so very craftily, to avoid arousing the suspicions of his colleagues. "My scream is the best way of masking my attitude," he often used to say, and everybody knew it. The Jews took to him and gave him their trust. He helped many of them to escape and to get their property out of the ghetto. Sometimes he escorted a Jew as a "prisoner", whereas in reality he was making it easier for them to cross the border. When times were hard he provided the Jews with bread and lard, which he personally brought to the posts. Of course, not all of these acts were selfless, but on some occasions they were. And yet he never did anything that could harm anyone. After the last deportation, many Jews were still hidden in the ghetto. Bousko knew many of the hiding places, and many a Jew owed his life to him. He also helped the Poles in many instances.

In July 1944, when the Germans were rapidly retreating to the east, Bousko was in danger of being called to the front. To prevent this, he self-administered intramuscular injections of propidon, which is an artificial

1 Engelbert Dollfuss, 14th Federal Chancellor of Austria (1932–1934).

method of triggering large boils. He developed a fever and the medical board sent him to hospital, where he spent a few months. When he realised he was riding a one-trick pony, he decided it was time to get off. He put on a disguise and ran away to somewhere near Kalwaria where he hid — so they said — with his Polish girlfriend, two Jewish children who were in his care, and a decent-sized suitcase full of valuables he had earned for his services during his time in the ghetto.

It wasn't long before Bousko's disappearance was discovered, and the chief of the German police in Podgórze launched a search. After all, this was at a time when the disappearance of German policemen was a frequent occurrence, as they were often taken hostage by Polish partisans. Bousko knew this, and decided to use it to his advantage. He wrote a letter to his commandant saying he'd been abducted and that he was now in the hands of the partisans, but that he didn't know where; what's more, even if he had known, they wouldn't have let him write down his whereabouts. His life depended on whether the Poles on the last list of persons sentenced to death had been killed or not. That letter was the beginning of his undoing. An intensive search was begun which lasted until he was captured (complete with beard) trying to cross the border. He was taken to Krakow and incarcerated at Montelupich prison. His attempt at feigning mental illness was in vain. The military court sentenced him to death and he was shot on 18 October 1944.

It took a long time for the Germans to calm down after Bousko's desertion was uncovered. They could not forgive themselves for having trusted him so much and for having been so greatly deceived. Now they suspected him of everything. They ascribed every Jewish escape from the ghetto to him. They attributed every unsuccessful German operation to him and claimed that he had been passing official secrets on to the Jews. Bousko's subordinates included two Viennese, a good-natured man called Essel, a shoemaker by profession, and Breczko, a degenerate and homosexual; Wita, a Volksdeutsch Silesian who was later arrested by the Germans for robbery; and Schubert, a wily devil who smuggled in the underground newspapers. All of them generally behaved decently.

The ghetto remained surrounded by the Sonderdienst. I returned to the pharmacy, this time accompanied by an officer from the Blue Police. We saw German guards marching in groups of four, their rifles at the ready. And sure enough, they fired occasional shots at the windows whenever they spotted someone.

Meanwhile in the ghetto, the German authorities issued an order demanding the renewal of all Kennkarten, regardless of whether or not they had an SS stamp. Everyone was to report to the building on Józefińska Street on Saturday, 6 June 1942. They were to bring their identification documents and Kennkarten in order to obtain a so-called Blauschein. Yet again, people stood from early morning, uncertainly and anxiously waiting for the result of their registration. The committee comprising Gestapo officers might issue or refuse to issue these little blue cards. Neither professional qualifications nor employment status were decisive in whether or not a card was issued. Those who did not receive one were held and shortly afterwards taken to the courtyard of the "Optima" factory[1] on Węgierska Street. They weren't allowed to take anything with them. OD men buzzed around among the Gestapo officers, maintaining order. Förster, Spira, Pacanower, Wertal and Süsser intervened — all in the service of the Gestapo. Their interventions, backed up by sums of money and gifts of gold and precious stones, were mainly effective. The Germans in charge of workshops also recommended their own employees who were eminent specialists. Their efforts were less effective, however, because they didn't have any persuasive backing.

A new announcement appeared warning that anyone caught without a Blauschein after a set deadline would be shot. As a matter of fact, every announcement, every order issued by the German authorities carried the threat of death. And so no wonder they no longer made much of an impression on anyone; quite the opposite — they prompted jokes. In those days you were considered lucky if you died a natural death in your own bed.

1 The courtyard at the "Optima" factory was where Jews earmarked for deportation were taken.

The courtyard at the "Optima" factory began to fill up with deportees. The weather, as if ironically, was fine again. The sun blazed and the air was stuffy and tiring. It was particularly unbearable for the elderly and the sick. Without water, and very often without a piece of bread, the Jews sat in the open air and awaited their fate. Despite having survived the two previous deportations, despite the many scenes they had witnessed, they couldn't take in the thought of what lay ahead of them. This was reflected in their requests to their relatives, relayed through the OD men, for warm clothing, money, soap and other such things. Interventions with the authorities made by the Judenrat, the OD and the commissioners continued.

Every so often someone would come into the pharmacy to ask for help for a relative waiting to leave in the "Optima" courtyard. The ladies working at the pharmacy had their hands full, giving out medicine, food and cigarettes. The good Dr Schlang and his wife, Dora, were also very active at this time.

And again we were able to obtain a few Blauscheine from Kunde — it was all down to chance, or to lucky coincidence, and nothing could be thought through or planned ahead. Thanks to those little blue cards, several of our friends returned to the ghetto; in the evening we drank to their miraculous rescue, and once again we were cheerful, if only for a few hours.

Now and then someone would leave the square, only to be replaced by new groups of people led by OD men from the building where the committee was operating.

The night from Saturday to Sunday was terrible. Members of the Sonderdienst carried out searches of those waiting in the "Optima" courtyard. They took anything of value. On the morning of Sunday 7 June, some new groups of people were brought in. I saw some venerable old men and women who could hardly move their legs, some seriously ill people who had been dragged from hospital, and I saw disabled people being supported as they walked to their ordeal.

Some people had already been sitting in the square for almost two days in the tremendous heat, with no food or water.

Monday 8 June came. The deportation began: people got up and listened to the calling and shouting of the German guards. The gates of the "Optima" courtyard were opened. The first deportees began to leave the courtyard; they were put in groups which were heavily guarded by the Sonderdienst. The Germans had their rifles cocked, ready to shoot at any moment. The procession moved along Limanowski Street and Wielicka Street towards the train station at Prokocim; once there, the new arrivals were loaded onto the waiting train. Many of the coaches already had deportees from Miechów, Jędrzejów and Słomniki on board. A small handful of people were saved from the Krakow transport, excluded by the Gestapo and sent to the "Julag", i.e. the forced labour camp in Płaszów.

The hospitals were emptied of their patients during the deportation too, so it is no surprise that during each

17. Sections of the wall
with a view of Krzemionki hill

action, anybody who could and who had the strength abandoned the hospital to go and hide in strangers' houses or other hiding places, wherever they could sit it out, and then return to the hospital later.

Unfortunately, somehow the Germans found out that the hospital was full again. They ordered three doctors — Dr Fischer, Dr Bornstein and Dr Engelstein — to make selections from among the patients in order to reduce their numbers to the minimum. This order was beyond human capability. Who could decide whether a particular patient should live or die? Who could take on such a responsibility? What premises could one possibly apply? Here I should stress the dignity shown by Dr Bornstein, despite the fact that one of the patients who couldn't move was his own mother. He did not attempt to save her at the expense of anyone else's life. Those who knew what happened behind the scenes felt great admiration for Dr Julian Aleksandrowicz, who bravely executed a daring plan thought up by his wife, Maryla. Aleksandrowicz deceived the Germans by moving out some of the disabled and people on stretchers and putting them in the long queue of people getting ready to leave the ghetto. Reporting to the Germans that their order had been carried out, he pointed to a small group of disabled people and patients on stretchers; the Germans concluded that the entire, bigger group were all patients moved out of the hospital. Once the Germans had left, the patients vanished into thin air, leaving the line of other people and hiding either in

18. Deportation of the Jews

private homes or in the corners of various cellars and attics, to sit it out until the deportation was over.

In the three stages of the first June deportation, seven thousand people were driven out of the ghetto. It later transpired that all the transports were headed for the Bełżec extermination camp.

The fate of the deportees became the main subject of conversation in the ghetto. Family members left behind tried by every means possible to get solid information about their relatives. They came up with all sorts of conjecture. The most improbable rumours began to spread, each one from "a highly reliable" source. The authors of these rumours were always so-called decent Germans, who were supposedly giving away the secrets of the German authorities. It was a well-known technique: just a way to dull people's vigilance, to give hope that the deportees were alive, anything to avoid pushing people to their limits, anything to prevent attempts to revolt.

Rumours circulated that the deportees had been sent to Ukraine to work on the land. Some German railwaymen were saying they had seen an enormous number of barracks with their own eyes, and in them were Jews from all over Europe. They were doing well, working hard but they had everything they needed, they were being given food and clothing. Of course they were heavily guarded, surrounded by barbed wire and nobody could go near there; they weren't allowed to write letters and so no news was coming from them. People showered these storytellers with requests to go there, to take messages from the ghetto and return with replies. Naturally, at first the Germans turned down these requests, saying they couldn't, that perhaps later; this was to make things seem as difficult as possible and by this token to increase the amount of compensation on offer. People didn't care about money, they paid whatever was being demanded simply to hold onto a glimmer of hope; yet nothing comforting or certain made its way into the ghetto. The Germans would take the money and then evaporate, while the people sat there trustfully waiting.

I knew a Pole called Tataruch who was married to a Jewish woman. She had been in the ghetto and had then been sent into the unknown. Her husband looked everywhere for her. He even went to Ukraine, but he found no trace of any barracks or Jews working there. Nobody could understand why entire trainloads of deportees were vanishing so mysteriously. And nobody could even make a rough guess where those transports were headed. It was only several months later that news began to reach the ghetto; that was when we first heard the names Bełżec, Majdanek and Treblinka — camps with tall, smoking crematory chimneys.

Nevertheless, thoughts of mass murder, choking gas and burning bodies in furnaces had not yet entered anyone's mind. But information was coming in more and more often about the atrocities taking place while people were being loaded onto the trains, about mysterious stations with no name, and dead-end tracks down which trains were travelling full of people, who were sometimes left waiting for days on end without food or water, only to disappear into dense forest surrounded by barbed wire, from beyond which no sound would ever be heard again. People speculated that the deportees were disappearing into secret factories where the Germans were producing new weaponry to use against their enemies; but in no case did anyone ever say that every last one of these people had gone to their death.

Until one sunny day, the news ran round the ghetto like wildfire that one single man from a transport bound for Bełżec had managed to escape and return to the ghetto. Who was this daredevil? And by what means had he alone, of so many thousands, managed to escape? What was he saying? And what about all the others? What fate lay ahead of them? The list of questions was endless... This daredevil turned out to be a dentist named Bachner. He had escaped from the transport. Staking everything on one card, he had dashed to the nearest free-standing latrine and jumped right into the sewage pit. He had spent several days in there, chest-deep in human excrement. Once the sounds of the deportees had faded away to silence, Bachner had slipped out of his terrible hiding place during the night and slowly, slowly made his way towards Krakow until he reached the ghetto, the starting point for his recent journey into the unknown.

And it was from him that the ghetto discovered the truth — that there were camps where the Germans were murdering, gassing and burning the transported prisoners. Bachner's stories were horrifying and difficult to take in. How on earth was it possible, in the twentieth century, for these people, who were known worldwide for so many great humanists, so many thinkers and philosophers, to have become so shamefully degraded?

Today, if we calmly reflect on the way in which the three June deportations were conducted, we can see the carefully planned duplicity employed by the Germans to mislead people, to rob them not only of their lives but also of all their personal possessions, and to facilitate this pillage through all those cleverly stylised orders.

The first deportation order sounded very innocent: because of overcrowding in the ghetto, wishing to provide better living conditions for the rest of the inhabitants and by the same token to avoid the danger of infectious diseases, the authorities were compelled to relocate part of the Jewish population. However, each of them was allowed to take with them as much as they could carry. Indeed, people took enormous quantities of luggage, but their first priority was to take the most valuable items because they assumed their fate would be the same as that of their predecessors, whom the Germans had taken to the Lublin region and set free. Or perhaps they'd be moved to another ghetto? They arrived at the first transports with nearly all their luggage. Their things were only taken from them once they had reached the station at Płaszów, but no body searches were carried out. Searches only took place once they had reached their destination. All this was done to convince people on the next transport that they could take small things with them, and that they should leave the larger items behind. The Germans knew perfectly well that in this case they would all take small, but valuable objects, such as jewellery, money and gold. During the second deportation, the Germans employed a different technique; they carried out body searches on the spot and pilfered whatever they could lay their hands on. Whatever they failed to find was taken by their colleagues when the deportees arrived at their destination. Larger bundles and suitcases were now regularly pillaged in Zgoda Square. Workers brought in from the Baudienst took away the items people had left at home.

During the third deportation, people without a blue card were detained on the spot and were not allowed to take anything from their homes. Their flats were then sealed by the OD.

On 10 June 1942, the German guards left the ghetto. The Jews, now mentally exhausted, heaved a sigh of relief. After a week of terror and uncertainty from one day to the next, they were nervous wrecks. Now they began to return to ostensible equilibrium, despite frequently occurring symptoms of mental breakdown. Many people sank into a state of apathy and resignation. A large number of suicides were reported during the three deportations, mainly through gassing or poisoning with potassium cyanide. At the start, getting one's hands on poison proved extremely difficult, but later a source was found: the Wachs lamp factory on Lwowska Street used cyanide in its production process. And that was mainly where people got hold of this substance, which was measured out in quantities many times the lethal dose and stored as if it were some priceless treasure. Entire families kept doses of the poison in small flasks which they carried about with them at all times just in case.

In the first few weeks following the deportation, many people looked for ways to get out of the ghetto. And indeed, a great many succeeded in doing so. Some of them escaped from the building where my pharmacy was located: Dr Oberlender and his family, Mr Jutkiewicz and his mother and sister, Mrs Feliksowa (the wife of the renowned Krakow doctor Józef Feliks) and her daughter. Dr R. Lachs also escaped with this group. Their escape from the ghetto and their journey to Warsaw was organised and facilitated by that mysterious and controversial figure, Aleksander Förster. Nearly all of these people were killed, either in the Warsaw Uprising, or sooner. For example, Natan Oberlender was killed by a bomb and his wife buried him in the courtyard of the building where they were living; she managed to survive the occupation and returned to Krakow, where we often used to meet.

Besides the extreme pessimists, there was no shortage of people in the ghetto who watched what was going on around them with an uncritical eye, people who were unable to draw any rational conclusions from the events they were witnessing, and there were those who continued to trust the Germans. With obsessive persistence, these people kept saying that the good Germans had assured them that the deportations were the final act in the Jewish tragedy. These voices mainly belonged to people who worked in German institutions, where the Germans circulated these lies, and the Jews would bring them back to the ghetto as unquestionable truths. But the majority of residents no longer had any faith in assurances of this kind.

A few days after the June deportation, a notice appeared announcing a reduction in the size of the ghetto. The following streets now lay outside the ghetto area: Rękawka Street, part of Krakus Street and Węgierska, the whole of Czarniecki Street (where the court and the prison were located) and the right-hand side of Limanowski Street (running off Podgórski Market Square). The Judenrat's housing office, headed by a lawyer named Dr Jakub Wasserlauf, was given the task of re-housing the remaining people. The now redundant sections of wall were partly demolished, then posts were driven into the ground and connected with thick barbed wire. The external appearance of the ghetto had somewhat altered: it was now more apparent from the "Aryan" side. Straight after the announcement of this new order, there was a new migration of people with furniture, similar to when the district was first established, only this time the pace was much quicker and more fraught with anxiety. From early morning till late at night people frantically ran along carrying possessions on their backs, hauling bundles of linen, suitcases, trunks and baskets, shifting items of furniture and priceless treasures, such as coal and wood. Only a small number of people were able to afford furniture trolleys and handcarts, which were extremely expensive. For several days there was an exceptional flurry of activity. The ghetto was living on its nerves and people were completely exhausted, both mentally and physically.

The resettlement was completed by the deadline imposed by the authorities. Life began to return to normal, but only ostensibly. Time passed, healing some of the wounds inflicted and partially numbing the painful void caused by the departure of so many loved ones. But the spark of life was not extinguished. Instead of giving up, people began to get organised again; shops which had closed down in those streets now cut off from the ghetto re-opened in new premises, and shops whose owners had been deported were often taken over by others. But the peace of earlier times never returned. Fear made people doubly vigilant. Every little thing aroused mistrust, and even the most innocent of orders from any authority whatsoever triggered endless discussion, speculation and predictions. Life was becoming increasingly difficult, the freedom of residents ever more restricted, the regulations allowing people to go out into the city were ever tougher, and obtaining a pass was harder and harder. The Arbeitsamt was working at full steam: there were new card indexes, new job assignments, and new checks on those working. The hospitals filled up with patients. More and more people were being worked to the bone, malnourished, physically abused and degraded — unsurprisingly there was an increase in rates of illness and suicide.

In the ghetto there were four hospitals: 1. the central hospital, which had been moved from Skawińska Street to the Jewish district, and was now located on the corner of Józefińska Street and Węgierska Street; the head of this hospital was Dr Nüssenfeld, a well-known surgeon; 2. the isolation hospital on Rękawka Street, expertly run by Dr A. Biberstein; after the ghetto was made smaller and Rękawka Street was excluded, the hospital moved to a small side street next to Zgoda Square; 3. a small geriatric hospital on Limanowski Street, run by a wonderful man called Dr Kranz, who died with his patients during the June deportation in 1942; and 4. a convalescent hospital on Józefińska Street, run by two highly knowledgeable and dedicated men — Dr Julian Aleksandrowicz and Dr Bornstein.

Throughout all the deportations and bloody actions, these hospitals played a huge role in hiding people by pretending they were gravely ill; there people found help, fictional diagnoses and some cleverly devised hiding places.

I visited all the hospitals in the ghetto and I went to nearly every single old people's home. I was impressed by the remarkable talent and selflessness of the hospital managers and their staff. I saw how the patients responded to Dr Aleksandrowicz with fondness and gratitude, I heard words of thanks addressed to Dr Kranz and his right hand, Mrs Gutmanowa. I was astonished by the central hospital on Józefińska Street, which had relocated from Skawińska Street (if you could call it a relocation — the Germans had only allowed them to take a scant amount of equipment). This restored and freshly painted building housed every department found in a regular hospital. The operating theatre was in constant use, with one operation after another, day and night. Working alongside the ghetto doctors (Dr Nüssenfeld, Dr Ferdynand Lewkowicz and Dr Blau) were surgeons from the city, who in exceptional circumstances were allowed to enter the ghetto on special passes in the initial phase of its existence. Professors Jan Glatzel and January Zubrzycki came in to perform operations on a number of occasions. Professors Tadeusz Tempka and Aleksander Oszacki and Dr Stanisław Łapiński were frequently seen at case management meetings. Dr Blasberg and Dr Glassner managed the department of internal medicine; the neurology department was run by Dr Bornstein; gynaecology by Dr R. Lachs; ophthalmology by Dr Mirowski and Dr Michał Schel; ENT by Dr Feliks Grünbaum and Dr Edward Mahauf; dermatology by Dr Rosenzweig and Dr Henryk Engelstein; and the X-ray department was headed by Dr Otto Schwarz and Dr Czesław Blühbaum. The head of the epidemiology hospital was Dr A. Biberstein, of whom his patients spoke with the highest acclaim. The head of sanitation was Dr Haber, who acted as a liaison between the German authorities and the department of sanitation.

As well as these heads of department, almost all the doctors worked selflessly at the hospital.

The pharmacy became a meeting point after every deportation. Everybody knew that whoever had survived would come straight to us: here the others would be waiting, this was where all those of our friends whom fate had saved from death would show up. Each of them told how they had got away, where they had hidden, and how they had survived. There was joy and desperation. Some were pleased they had survived, others were numb with pain at the loss of their loved ones who would never return. The rest suffered pangs of remorse; they couldn't forgive themselves for ever having caused their loved ones pain, assuring themselves they hadn't meant it and that those momentary misunderstandings were the result of their anxious lifestyle and the constant fear of death. Their agony grew more intense by the moment. The mood was ghastly, people spoke in whispers and couldn't raise their heads for weeping. The sensation was like listening to the clatter of train wheels against tracks leading to nowhere. And so we all remained within our friends' silent mood of despair. Never again would the pharmacy door be pushed open by the hands of our friends and frequent guests, such as Dr Stanisław Eibenschutz, Dr Dora Haber, Dr Maurycy Haber, or Dr Dora Silbergerowa. They were gone forever.

The Judenrat had a tough job. I have already mentioned Commissioner Gutter. I also became better acquainted with a councillor, a Doctor of Law named

Streimer. Streimer was in his mid-fifties, a dangerously intelligent (and perhaps devious) man who was thoroughly educated and fluent in several languages. I spoke to him about general matters on several occasions, but Mr Schor had warned me beforehand to be exceptionally careful with him because his relationship with the Germans was unclear. I therefore attempted to conduct the conversation in a way that would let me find out for myself how much truth there was in these suspicions. The views he expressed were always thoroughly well-considered. He clearly had ready-made answers on many current topics. He would weigh each word carefully, skilfully selecting his expressions, never uttering a sentence too many. I couldn't find out anything for sure; his statements, particularly on political matters, always ended in two possible conclusions. Dr Streimer was an exceptionally self-assured individual who boasted about his familiarity with the German mentality and his ability to cope with Germans. He was tough, tenacious, and never smiled. He had a gloomy face and was a rather unpleasant person. He was shot by the Germans at the camp in Płaszów. Who he really was and what role he played in the ghetto remains a mystery which he took with him to the grave.

One of the longest-serving members of the Judenrat, who worked there almost from the very start, was a fellow pharmacist and old friend of mine, Leon Salpeter. Salpeter was idealistic, quiet, calm, level-headed and suave. When I asked him on a number of occasions why he didn't escape from the ghetto, his reply was always the same: even though he had the opportunity and could do it, he never would — he would stay there with everyone to the end. And he stuck to his decision. He stayed, and he survived to see the German defeat. Right after the war, he took part in the World Zionist Conference in London as a member of the delegation of Polish Jews. He moved to Jaffa, Israel, where he started up his own pharmacy. During my visit to Israel in 1957, I was a regular guest at the home of Mr and Mrs Salpeter. Leon's wife, the lovely Elizabeth, did everything she could to make my stay in their home as pleasant as possible. In 1967 we met again in Kiel for Kunde's trial. Kunde didn't live to receive his sentence; he died of cancer soon after. Poor Leon Salpeter passed away after undergoing a difficult operation in 1968.

Another member of the Judenrat was a councillor called Salomonowicz. He was about fifty-seven, a calm and wise man who gave everyone sound advice, and an unquestionably decent human being who helped wherever he could. He was able to talk to the Germans, and his interventions saved several lives during the June deportation.

For honest people, working at the Judenrat was very unpleasant. They had to carry out orders against their will, circumvent the law, play for time, and find enough self-control and composure to convince thousands of people that the Judenrat was not issuing the orders, but merely carrying them out on behalf of the Germans, none of which was easy. Many people held a hostile view of the Judenrat's activity in the ghetto, but nobody could accuse any of its members of anything in particular (there were, of course, a small number of exceptions). After the war I often heard the opinion that those who held, as it were, senior positions during the occupation should have resigned. One forgets, however, that resigning from such a position was as good as signing a death warrant for yourself and your family. And even then, somebody else would have had to fill those positions. Was it not better that those sitting on the Judenrat were, for the most part, decent people, rather than having their places filled by individuals in the service of the Germans? While being a hero and sacrificing oneself for an idea is undoubtedly a beautiful thing, it is a quality you have to be born with. And just as not everybody is born a genius, not everybody can be a hero either. Not everyone is capable of sacrificing his own life. So it is, always has been and always will be. Besides, I think the most interesting thing is that these accusations directed at members of the Judenrat were only made after the war, when people quickly began to forget the atmosphere and the circumstances of life in the ghetto. And most of the accusations came from people who were living far away from Poland during the occupation and who had never experienced the deportations or the atmosphere of terror prevalent in those situations. They simply weren't familiar with the Germans or the occupation at first hand. I am personally convinced that if there hadn't been so many honest and reliable people on the Judenrat, the fate of the ghetto residents would have been even more tragic, if it is at all possible to grade human tragedy.

Many of those who survived the war far away from Poland do not appreciate what the horror of the ghetto was like. When I was in America in 1965, I met a dear friend who had sat next to me at school. On the first day of our meeting — and bear in mind that my friend was Jewish — the conversation turned to my recollections of the Krakow ghetto.

"Tadeusz," he said, "I've been reading your little book, and I did like it, but I think your descriptions of the murder and harassment the Germans are supposed to have perpetrated against the Jews are a little exaggerated. Never mind — you got carried away with your imagination, you're entitled to do so. We all know the truth anyway."

"Henryk," I said, "where were you living at the time? On which planet? You don't believe me? I was in the ghetto throughout its entire existence, I lived there with those people. I was an eyewitness, as were the ladies who worked at my pharmacy — we saw everything that happened on Zgoda Square during the deportations, and not only there... and you talk about exaggeration..."

Further explanations were unsuccessful. After a while, he patted me on the shoulder and with a faint smile he said: "Let's forget about these sad matters and drink a toast to our past, our present and our future."

I haven't forgotten that conversation, and I keep asking myself just how many people there are in the world who think as he does.

The German authorities undoubtedly treated the Judenrat far worse than they did the OD. The personal benefits the Judenrat brought them were unquestionably smaller, and that was what the Germans valued the most. It isn't really possible to speak of trust on the part of the Gestapo towards the Judenrat, whereas trust did to some extent exist in relation to the OD as a whole, to say nothing of a few individuals who were blind devotees. The head of the OD, Spira, knew all about the German authorities' attitude to the Judenrat. He was forever stressing his own sense of superiority, while waging initially silent, but later open war against the council and its president, Rosenzweig, and then his successor, Commissioner Gutter. Spira emerged the victor from every skirmish with Gutter. The two of them were outwardly very alike: thin, shrivelled, and sickly-looking. And they had similar psychological traits too: they were exceedingly nervous, impulsive, degenerate, pathological types, seized by excessive ambition and an unbridled sexual excitability which was manifest in one brief erotic adventure after another. Gutter was more intelligent than Spira, and he had a gift for words and a smooth way of dealing with people that seemed to impress them. The Gestapo consolidated Spira's belief in his own power and fuelled his superiority complex. Spira and a few of his remaining close colleagues also profited from a large number of privileges which were denied every other Jew. He could leave the ghetto, walk about without an armband, travel around in hackney cabs and freely enter the Gestapo building. He knew nearly all the Gestapo officers, and they knew him well too. He knew how to present gifts for any trifling thing, for the smallest favour. Spira's adoration for his immediate boss, Kunde, knew no bounds. One could often hear the following statement from Spira's lips: "Of all people, only Spira will survive the war; everyone else will die, but he will live". And he was partly right. People live and die as a matter of course, and the names of even the most distinguished disappear into oblivion. But the name Spira will not vanish from human memory. Every chronicle, every memoir and every note about the Krakow ghetto will mention Symche Spira, a glazier in days of yore — and in the ghetto the head of the OD, the master of life and death for some fifteen thousand Jews.

The days and months went by, fraught with constant worries and problems. The cramped housing conditions made life more and more of a misery. In the second half of October 1942, the Germans issued an order concerning the latest ghetto reduction: residents of the district known as "Ukraine", i.e. the streets to the left of Lwowska Street, were given just one day to leave their homes and move to the remaining part of the ghetto. People were overcome with despair. The move began; nobody took furniture anymore, only everyday necessities. But then something miraculous happened — for the first time in the history of the ghetto they managed to get the German authorities to reverse their decision. The order was called off. The Jews gathered their things

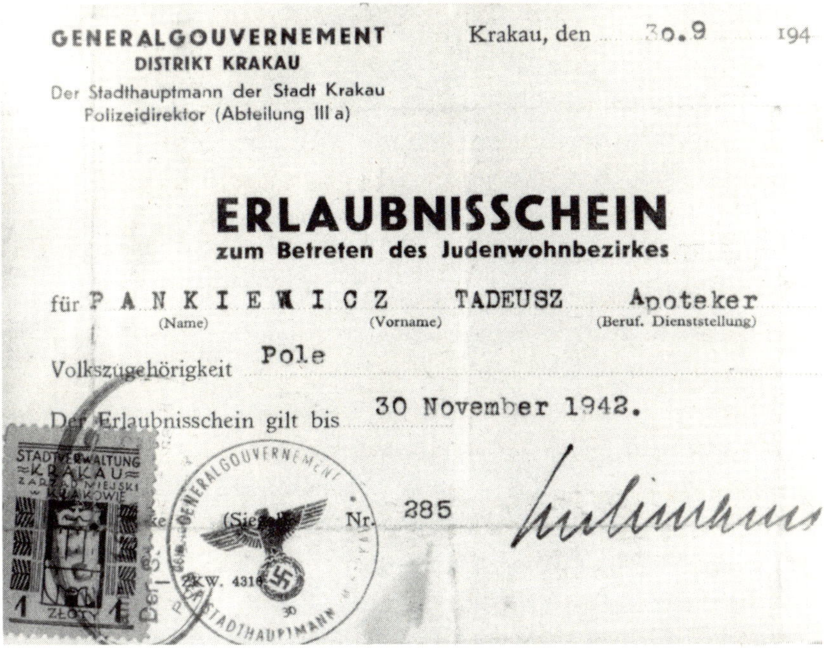

GENERALGOUVERNEMENT
DISTRIKT KRAKAU
Der Stadthauptmann der Stadt Krakau
Polizeidirektor (Abteilung III a)

Krakau, den 30.9 194

ERLAUBNISSCHEIN
zum Betreten des Judenwohnbezirkes

für P A N K I E W I C Z (Name) TADEUSZ (Vorname) Apoteker (Beruf. Dienststellung)

Volkszugehörigkeit Pole

Der Erlaubnisschein gilt bis 30 November 1942.

(Siegel) Nr. 285

STADTVERWALTUNG KRAKAU
1 ZŁOTY 1

GENERALGOUVERNEMENT
STADTHAUPTMANN

19. A permit to enter the ghetto,
issued to Tadeusz Pankiewicz in 1942

and returned to their abandoned homes. What joy! This event prompted all sorts of comment. However, a horrible disappointment lay just around the corner for the ghetto inhabitants.

I remember a typical incident from that period. It happened just a few months after the June deportation, when the cruel and savage scenes perpetrated by the Germans upon the defenceless population were still fresh in everyone's memory.

One morning a long column of German vehicles came through Zgoda Square, moving in the direction of Limanowski Street — a military column travelling swiftly eastwards. One of the vehicles knocked over a young Jewish boy who was running across the road. The car stopped, as did the long line of vehicles behind it. Someone picked the boy up and took him to hospital. The telephone in the local OD office was used to inform the German police on Franciszkańska Street. The German police came and began to investigate, with police officers measuring distances and asking at what speed the car had been going. Finally, they wrote out a report, and after almost an hour at a standstill, the vehicles moved on. I could not fully understand this, with the deaths of so many people still fresh in my mind. This was just mindless adherence to the rules, unparalleled bureaucracy, plain and simple! In any case, the boy was just bruised and quickly recovered; he returned to full health, only to lose his life in the first operation in which mass murder was exempt from legal scrutiny.

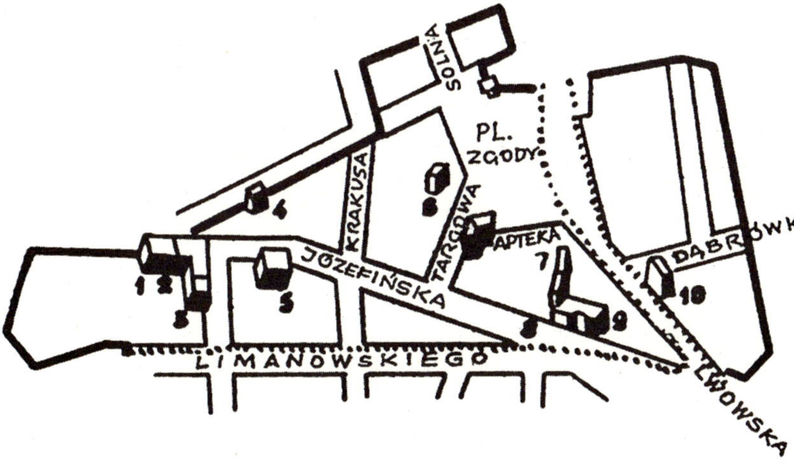

20. A map of the ghetto after the October deportation:
1. Arbeitsamt; 2. Hospital; 3. Council; 4. Bathhouse;
5. Jewish Social Aid (JUS); 6. Hospital for Infectious Diseases;
7. Prison; 8. Jewish Police (OD); 9. Dormitory; 10. OD building

Days passed, each one similar to the next, all equally tiring and equally uncertain. People returned to the ghetto each day from various workplaces with all manner of news and rumours concerning the fate of the ghetto. Once again there was talk of another deportation — later, of the complete liquidation of the ghetto. There was talk of Płaszów, and of a closed camp outside the ghetto walls. The Germans categorically denied this, and that worried people the most. Everyone thought the situation must definitely be different from the way the SS and Gestapo presented it. And they soon found out that it was the only correct line of thought. Whenever the Arbeitsamt began to organise and supplement its card indexes, it prompted grave fears among the ghetto population that there was something bad in the air.

The mood in the ghetto was getting worse from one day to the next. Day broke on 27 October 1942. By now everybody knew there was going to be another deportation the following day. Spira left the ghetto several times in a hackney cab. Each time he returned he was gloomy and extremely agitated, yet said nothing; he didn't even divulge the content of his conversations with the Gestapo authorities to his family. More and more Gestapo officers were appearing on the streets of the ghetto, all heading for the building housing the Jewish police, where the Germans who were closely involved in ghetto affairs had their own separate offices. This included three officers for Jewish affairs (a branch of the Sicherheitspolizei): SS-Obersturmführer Becher,

SS-Oberscharführer Siebert and Untersturmführer Brand. These men would only show up in the ghetto from time to time. The following officers were permanently stationed there: SS-Sturmscharführer Kriminalsekretär Wilhelm Kunde, Olde, and SS-Obersturmführer Hermann Heinrich.

The officers for Jewish affairs from the Gestapo were: SS-Obersturmführer Theodor Heinemayer, and Sipo officers Körner and Mallotke. From the SS und Polizei: SS-Oberführer Scherner, Sturmbannführer Haase, SS-Unterscharführer Horst Pilarzik, SS-Rottenführer Wiktor Ritschek and SS-Rottenführer Zugsberger.

Gutter went to the SS headquarters on Oleandry Street several times that day. He spoke to Oberführer SS und Polizeiführer Scherner, the highest-ranking authority for Jewish affairs in the Krakow district. The outcome of this decisive meeting was unfavourable; Gutter's alleged attempts to postpone the deportation deadline came to nothing.

On pain of death, Gutter was forbidden to mention the operation due to take place the following day. He returned to the ghetto, but was unable to keep the secret. In a matter of minutes the entire ghetto knew what to expect the next day. People began preparing in earnest for the impending operation. Everyone knew from experience that if you didn't have a stamp, you could hide for a short time during the deportation and use a variety of means to get a stamp later on; nobody would bother to check whether the stamp was authentic or not. Experience had taught that you needn't worry too much about the orders issued by the German authorities, with their incessant death threats. People were becoming fatalists, putting their destiny in the hands of fate. For some, the fate of the deportees was clear, and so they would sabotage the authorities' orders: "If I succeed, then good; if not, I'll die. I'll have to die sooner or later, anyway. Of the two possible options, I'd rather hide".

People rushed to find themselves a hiding place. Those with the opportunity and strong enough nerves to be able to hold out for a dozen or so hours in an uncomfortable position while listening to screaming Germans all around them, seemingly vanished from the ghetto, hidden away in the most ingeniously conceived places. People found hiding places in cellars, in attics, and in flats. I remember how a woman I knew concealed her parents in a pantry in the hall. She removed the shelves and covered the opening with a wooden panel with coat hooks and a mirror attached to it, the sort one normally finds in modern homes. She then nailed the panel to the wall. During the operation, the Germans searched the flat thoroughly and it didn't even enter their minds that somebody could be hiding behind the coat hooks.

Many people escaped into the city and stayed with close friends for a few days. Once the operation was over, they returned to the ghetto. I met several of them in town and I talked to them. In the case of Dr Nattlowa,

I was able to find her a room on Mikołajska Street, where she hid until the end of the action (which, incidentally, only lasted a day).

I returned to the ghetto at around 5 p.m. The mood there was one of dejection. Groups of anxious people gathered in the streets, debating what would happen to them next. Nobody doubted there would be a deportation the next day. With each passing hour their anxiety grew. Women, terrified for their children, were walking around in a trance-like state. The pharmacy was full; the only drugs we sold were tranquilisers, for which almost nobody had a prescription. Who would have thought of going to a doctor, when they doubted they'd be alive the next day? At about eight in the evening, the residents were informed by workers returning from town and officers of the Blue Police that a large, fully armed Sonderdienst unit was walking along the streets of Krakow towards Podgórze. The pharmacy was full of friends; the married with children were asking what to do. The doctors (who were supposedly to be protected) and the single people were generally calm.

At about nine o'clock that night the Sonderdienst unit came near to the walls of the ghetto, forming a cordon of armed soldiers around it: escape was now out of the question. It was a long, tiring, sleepless night. Nobody knew what criteria the Germans would employ this time when making their selections. People took food to their chosen hiding places. Every now and then someone would come into the pharmacy to ask for child doses of Luminal, a sedative. Why? It was given to small children and babies to prevent them from crying out and giving away their hiding places. That same day, i.e. late that night, another order was issued, mainly relayed verbally by the Judenrat. It ordered all workers to line up according to place of work in front of the Judenrat building early the following day, 28 October. The night of 27 October was terrible indeed. From evening until dawn the next day, many of our friends stayed with us in the pharmacy. There was a great deal of anxiety and the atmosphere was ghastly. People would come in to confer with others, then leave, only to show up again a few hours later. No one slept a wink that night. The pharmacy emptied before dawn and I was left alone. I realised my colleagues would be unable to get to the pharmacy that day. The reinforced police patrols were not letting anyone in unless they had special permission from the Gestapo.

The twenty-eighth of October was a lovely, spring-like day. The cloudless sky reminded me of the days of the June deportation. People gathered in front of the Judenrat building next to the entrance gate on Węgierska Street. Many of the people going to work had small children with them: they were hoping they'd be able to take their children with them and, if need be, the German commissioners would intercede for them with the police authorities.

From six o'clock in the morning, cars carrying SS and Gestapo dignitaries began to arrive in the ghetto. One of those who came was SS-Sturmbahnführer Haase, a tall, thin man of around forty, although he looked much older. He had grey hair, piercing steel-grey eyes, and he never laughed. He was married with four children, the youngest of whom was two years old. Haase was personally responsible for managing the October deportation.

As well as the SS and Gestapo officers, Arbeitsamt officials and "guests" from the administration, the managers of various German companies which employed Jews had also come, to try to get exemptions for specialist workers who had been selected for deportation. There were incidences of genuine compassion, and a willingness to help individual Jews, as I could tell from the accounts of directly interested parties. Each of these Germans usually acted out of self-interest in such cases; after all, the loss of staff, often including first-rate specialists, could lead to their workshops being closed down and everything that came after — the managers being sent to the front. So it was in their interests to save Jews from deportation.

The workers lined up to march out in front of the gate on Węgierska Street. Gestapo and SS officers started making their selections, but without applying any criteria at all. Age, posture and appearance decided whether a Gestapo officer's hand signal would send you through the gate or keep you in the ghetto. In rare cases, the managers were able to get the Gestapo officers to change their minds. Loud shouts were heard as the names of those being detained in the ghetto were called, meaning that these individuals were being excluded from the two groups. All this took place amid the incredible yelling of the Germans. Every now and then their whips lashed bodies in the crowd. Gutter, officials from the Judenrat, Spira and his staff were running from one German to another. Only a small number of them managed to sneak back some of the children that had been taken away, by taking advantage of the Gestapo's inattention. On the whole, the children were being pushed away from their parents.

The workers left the ghetto. Two ranks of fully armed Sonderdienst units came inside it and stopped on Zgoda Square. They stacked their rifles up against each other. Then, from Józefińska Street and from the direction of Lwowska Street, came the steady pounding footsteps of marching German police units. They were joined by heavily armed *šauliai*, Lithuanian and Latvian collaborators who served in German units and who were especially renowned for their cruelty and sadism. They were brought in during the liquidation of the ghetto.

I was alone in the pharmacy. None of my staff were allowed to enter the ghetto that day. I did not open the pharmacy; instead, I hung up a sign telling people to ring if they needed anything. I stood in my room, about a metre from the window so I wouldn't be spotted by the Germans standing directly below. The Germans issued an order for all ghetto residents to leave their homes by ten o'clock in the morning, and to proceed to Józefińska Street; there they were to line up in the section between the Judenrat building and the OD building. Anyone found in their homes after ten o'clock would immediately be shot.

Crowds of people left their flats, which they had been instructed to leave unlocked. Józefińska Street was soon very crowded. SS and Gestapo officials briefly inspected their papers and, with a wave of the hand, sentenced some to deportation, and others to remain in the ghetto. Again, no criteria were used: pot luck, caprice and chance decided everything. Doctors and members of the Judenrat wore special armbands which were supposed to protect them from deportation and give them freedom of movement (of which they only took advantage in exceptional circumstances). The doctors were supposed to gather at the hospital. As it turned out, their armbands did not help them. With my own eyes I saw Germans taking people with armbands away for deportation if they didn't like the look of them. I watched as they forced a pharmacist named Immerglück and his wife onto a transport, even though they were members of the sanitation board. Their efforts to explain and to show their documents were futile. The German calmly took their papers and tore them up without reading them. I saw one German kicking Dr Zygmunt Leinkram as he pushed him into the crowd of deportees.

More people kept running into the square, beaten and pushed along by rifle butts amid the constant screaming of the SS men. Haase wanted to bring it about so that all the Jews would emerge from their cleverly constructed hiding places. He walked out onto a platform among the buildings and raised his hand. There was deathly silence. Then he said: "*Alle Männer und Frauen gehen ruhig nach Hause...*" ("All men and women should quietly go home..."). The deathly silence was broken by shouts of joy from the hundreds of people who heard those words. But their joy was short-lived. Haase's hand went up again, which was again followed by deathly silence. And then came more German words: "*...um ihre notwendigste Sachen mitzunehmen. Ghetto ist judenrein!*"[1] ("...to collect their most essential items — the ghetto is free of Jews!"). And now everything became clear. In a flash the news spread through the entire ghetto, creeping into every house, every room, and reaching even the most secret hiding places. A great many people were taken in by this lie and came out of hiding to share the fate of the others. The children of the well-known Weintraub family left their hideout. Their desperate parents had hidden them in pieces of furniture which were loaded onto carts heading for the camp at Płaszów (which was speedily being built), where they were hidden in one of the barracks under construction. Unfortunately, they didn't last long in their new shelter. Some vile traitors quickly informed the Germans about the concealed children, all of whom were shot soon after. This was by no means an isolated incident. One of the informers, a woman named

1 *Judenrein* (Ger.), lit. "clean of Jews".

Chilowiczowa, was given the task of detecting children hidden within the camp and reporting what she found to the Germans. As a result, they frequently shot not only the children, but also their parents.

The first shots rang out in the ghetto and the first victims of the October deportation fell in the courtyards, hallways and pavements. Some lay wounded, others were pouring with blood, yet others were dead. The Nazi executioners watched the horrendous death throes of their victims. There was a wall of silence on both sides. The crowd on the square kept growing from one minute to the next. Those who were standing were ordered to sit down. Nobody was allowed to stand up, not even to perform bodily functions. The people were impossibly packed together, with no water. This time there were no doctors on the square, nobody to come and help, though the heat was stifling. Those Dantean scenes will remain forever in the memories of all those who witnessed or experienced it, as I did.

It is easy to imagine what must have been happening to those who had gone out to work, who had no idea about the events taking place in the ghetto. They were consoled by the Germans' assurances that their families would be protected. The workers were mainly men; their wives, children and parents were deported without the opportunity of saying farewell to their loved ones. The deportees also included old people taken from nursing homes, people from hospices and patients from hospitals, who had been ordered to remain in their beds.

At around noon, SS men entered the main hospital on Józefińska Street and shot any patients who couldn't run away. The Germans beat anyone they came across in the hallways, and drove out the hospital staff; they didn't even show respect for a woman who was in labour, but had her thrown onto a trolley standing in front of the hospital, which was designated for those patients whom they didn't manage to kill on the spot. The order was carried out. At least a dozen doctors lost their lives in that operation.

Meanwhile, SS and Gestapo officers of various ranks were buzzing about in the square. Nearly all of them carried a whip or a stick, and there were even quite a few wielding pokers, which complemented the *Totenkopf*[1] insignia on their caps perfectly. All those sticks and rods rained down on the heads and bodies of those standing in the square, irrespective of age or gender. Older men and women were treated particularly brutally. At the sight of the beaten and bloody Jews, the majority of the Germans burst out laughing.

There were also those who didn't laugh. Standing right in front of my window was an SS man, a captain by rank. He was in his mid-forties, handsome, with a dark complexion and hair which was greying at the temples. He didn't go over to the group of SS and Gestapo

1 *Totenkopf* (Ger.), lit. "death's head", the skull and crossbones symbol on the uniform of the SS.

dignitaries standing in the middle of the square. He stood there, nervously smoking cigarettes, lighting one after another and frequently discarding a half-smoked cigarette before fetching out another. He caught my attention because he was partially blocking my view of the square. He was extremely upset. Next to him stood an exceedingly tall SS sergeant who was cackling incessantly; he kept saying things to his comrade and pointing at blood-stained and beaten people. The officer didn't smile even once, nor did he utter a word. After a while he walked up to Haase, exchanged a few words with him, saluted and then left the ghetto.

The shooting increased with every minute. More groups were brought into the square. The deportees were bunched together more and more tightly. The heat was unbearable; practically nobody was wearing a hat or carrying a parcel. They had been taken away just as they were. There were also those — I was told later — who had deliberately taken nothing with them, to avoid tiring themselves on what was possibly the last journey they would ever make. This time, however, a significant percentage of Jews realised what lay ahead. They no longer believed in the "Ukraine" myth and the camps of Jews living there.

After ten o'clock, in accordance with a newly issued order, Sonderdienst and SS patrols began to search flats, attics and cellars. Touring each building in groups of four, they used axes to break down locked doors. Shots kept resounding, as well as the noise of dogs howling as they ran across the packed square, names being screamed, moans, sobs and wails as people said their final goodbyes, as they were parted from the elderly parents and children they were not allowed to take with them. This was a hell nobody could ever forget. The old people, particularly the old men, as well as carrying small bundles, had prayer books in embroidered velvet bags tucked under their arms. Their faith and piety were undiminished. Some whispered the words: "God, where are you?" Others replied: "He is here". And then came the response, said with a gentle smile: "God is on leave, but He shall return".

The Germans screamed over the heads of the people sitting there. Now and then someone in the crowd tried to say something to one of the guards, to explain something. Every such attempt met with a punch, a rifle butt or a hard kick. The tall, stiff figure of Major Haase reigned over them all. As still as a statue, he surveyed the proceedings, surrounded by a team of Gestapo and SS men — the master not of life, but of death.

The faces of so many good friends passed before my eyes. I saw people with whom I had had long conversations; I saw those who during our political discussions had been tenacious optimists, and I saw their pessimistic opponents. The rich and the poor, the young and the old, men, women and children stood side by side, all crammed together. I saw the wife of Dr Tiger (my neighbour for many years before the war), standing there with her son; she was wearing a summer dress, but didn't have a coat or any luggage. I saw Dr Leon Glück with his wife and daughter. He was pulled off the transport at the last minute, but his wife and daughter went. I saw Wachs, the industrialist whom I mentioned earlier when I wrote about the political discussions he used to have with Dr Oberlender. I saw our daily visitor, Filip Schor. And I saw many doctors: Fryderyka Ameisen, Adolf Diestler, Fuchs-Katzowa, Amalia Goldman, Rachela Molkner, Adolf Kaiser, Gizela Gutmann, Barbara Rosenbaum, Zygmunt Leinkram, Stefania Silberger, Ida Sperling, Stiglitz-Straucherowa, Jakub Weinstein, Wanda Zaks, and Jakub Zabner. Dr Jakub Franz, who ran the little hospital on Limanowski Street, died heroically during the deportation, alongside his seriously ill patients. It is impossible to list all the friends and acquaintances who were standing in the square, awaiting an unknown future.

Meanwhile the Sonderdienst and SS patrols were going from building to building, looking for people in hiding. I could hear their axes smashing through doors and the bang of gun shots. I sat alone in the locked pharmacy. The Germans' booming voices and the clatter of heavy, hobnailed boots were getting closer and closer. Their terrifying, piercing voices rang in my ears. To avoid being shot, I hid behind the door frame. By now I could hear the footsteps of these so-called soldiers just a few metres away from the pharmacy door.

The Germans divided their activities in the following way: one of them went up to the attic, a second to the other end of the hallway, a third to the cellar, and the fourth stood just outside the door leading from the lobby into the pharmacy. He fired a shot from his rifle, probably to give himself courage. The gunshot echoed noisily around the empty lobby of the deserted building. As a first target he chose the door opposite my room. Unable to open it, he set about trying to smash it. When I heard the crack of breaking wood, I decided to come out. I opened the door and, in the semi-darkness, saw a short, stocky German struggling to do his job. He didn't notice me, nor did he hear my footsteps. I tapped him on the back and said: "*Verzeihen*" ("Excuse me"). As if electrocuted, he turned around in terror; he obviously couldn't fathom how somebody could have got here, since the order had clearly stated that anyone caught in a building after ten o'clock would be shot. I stood opposite him in my white pharmacist's coat, which I had put on deliberately to demonstrate the reason for my presence. But without waiting for my explanation he saluted, turned round and hurriedly walked away.

I returned to my room. Barely five minutes had gone by when I heard the sound of footsteps and the loud voices of several Germans. They were coming towards my door. There was a loud kick at the door, and I opened it. In came an SS officer, a non-commissioned officer and two privates. They asked me why I was there. I showed them all the relevant documents, which they looked through with only mild interest. The non-commissioned officer explained that the order was explicit and that there could be no exceptions. On hearing the firm tone of his subordinate, the officer — perhaps out of sheer contrariness — started proving to him that my papers were actually in order. In spite of my explanations, they took me with them. I left the pharmacy and was led over to a group of Jews standing in the square. The Germans then left.

Meanwhile, ever larger groups of people were being brought in from every nook and cranny in the ghetto. The OD men scuttled about, standing to attention and receiving orders. Spira stood as stiff as a poker in front of a high-ranking Gestapo officer, while Pacanower and Gutter obsequiously hovered nearby. Förster moved around freely, with his hands in his pockets and no band on his arm. From time to time he would appeal to the Germans. Sometimes his interventions were successful: the Germans would allow this man or that to be excluded from the transport. This was followed by frenzied thanks, as those who had been rescued threw their arms around their patrons' necks and cried with joy.

I stood there and awaited judgment. I shivered at the thought that the deportation could begin at any minute and then nothing would be able to save me. After a while, SS-Sturmbannführer Haase appeared, accompanied by the officer who had examined my papers in the pharmacy. The lieutenant beckoned to me. The guard let me through, and I went up to Haase, explained my presence, and showed him my papers. Those seconds seemed to last a lifetime; just a nod of the head or one little word — "*nein*" —and I would have shared the fate of the Jews. Haase said: "I know about this" and signalled for me to be released.

I returned to the pharmacy feeling as if I had been to hell and back. I was utterly exhausted. I took up my previous observation post, a metre away from the window draped with a net curtain.

Then I saw a scene I shall never forget as long as I live. Thousands of people were standing or sitting in Zgoda Square. About fifteen paces away from them stood a group of high-ranking SS men and Gestapo officers, in superbly-cut uniforms and shiny jack boots, with whips, sticks and pokers in their hands. They were laughing and mocking incessantly; now and then they would approach a group of Jews and give vent to their violent urges by kicking and hitting them. Many of them had flushed faces, burning with ardour. Suddenly, a Jewish woman with a small child at her breast threw herself at the feet of an SS man and began to plead for her life. Gutter was standing next to this SS man. The woman wept, cried out and begged Gutter for help, saying her name over and over again and stating her husband's occupation. But nothing helped; the SS man kicked her brutally and walked away. Refusing to give up, the woman ran after him, grabbed Gutter by the hand and begged him again. The German turned around and struck her across the head several times with his whip. The anxious Gutter pushed her away, screaming at her pitilessly. The unfortunate woman fell to the ground unconscious. One of the Sonderdienst guards came up, grabbed her by the hand and dragged her and her child back to the group. That was the only time I ever witnessed one of the Jews publicly begging a German for mercy.

While this incident was taking place, something else was happening too. I saw a pretty young woman walking slowly and majestically across the empty space between the pharmacy and the group of SS men. She was beautifully dressed and wore a light-green rubber cape. She came close to the SS men, and without looking at them continued on her way, clearly heading towards the crowd of deportees. It later transpired that her mother was standing there. The surprised Germans goggled after her. One of them — the fattest one with the reddest face — folded his hands, holding a riding crop, behind his back and walked up to her. He had a slight stoop and a wild expression on his face, his eyes burning with fury. The woman stopped, he said something, and she replied, then suddenly he began to hit her. He kept hitting her like mad across the face, the eyes, hair, neck and back. I could hear each blow from my room in the pharmacy, because there was a deathly silence. The woman bowed her head slightly and remained motionless, like a statue. She wanted to be deported voluntarily, to be with her mother, and this had provoked the SS man's fury. Not a single groan came out of her, she didn't cry or beg. The German was unable to break her, unable to force her to beg and plead. He angrily pushed her towards the deportees, kicking and hitting her the whole time. She stood next to her mother, but neither of them spoke a word to each other. The SS man walked away, and the woman took out a tissue and wiped her face; her mother stroked her head and dried her tears. A few minutes passed. The German approached her again and said something to her. I couldn't see whether she responded or not, because she had her head down. Then the German grabbed her by the hair and pulled her out of the line, beating her and screaming horribly, before pointing his riding crop to show which way she was to go. She was not allowed to stay with her mother, she had to go on living. That was the will of the SS. The woman slowly walked away, powerless in the face of such violence, as her mother gazed after her for the very last time.

And thus the Germans were not fated to hear wailing, complaints and cries of despair in the Krakow ghetto, and this must — in my opinion — have angered them most of all. Their victims' silence drove them mad.

This scene didn't make the slightest impression on the other SS men who witnessed it. They watched it as if it was the most normal thing in the world, as if this sort of behaviour were a generally accepted way of treating people.

It was almost time for the march to begin. Many people — there were around two thousand there — had left their hiding places and come outside to be with their loved ones. Those who stayed behind survived this time.

Many sick and disabled people were eliminated during the October deportation, dragged out of hospitals and hospices. Almost all the residents in the old people's home on Limanowski Street (run by Dr Kranz) were killed; the orphanage and the boarding school both fell victim to German crimes, and children were taken from the hospital for infectious diseases. Prisoners from the OD jail, from Montelupich prison and the nearest concentration camps were also added to the group of deportees. The Germans were especially cruel towards patients in the hospital attached to the nursing home on Limanowski Street. Elderly men and women — most of whom were disabled — were dragged from their beds and herded along the corridors towards the stairs amid dreadful screaming. Whipped and pushed, most of them shed blood. I needn't explain how they got downstairs: as Dr Kranz told me later, not one of them descended in the normal manner. Most of them collapsed on the stairs and tumbled to the bottom. The Germans kicked away their crutches and tripped them up; these stunts were accompanied by the usual laughter. In the courtyard, they were lined up against a wall and ordered to jump up and down. There, as the Germans laughed, they were shot. It wasn't easy to die a natural death in the ghetto.

During the deportation many people committed suicide. Several elderly people urgently asked their loved ones to give them poison. One of the ghetto's renowned doctors, a radiologist named Dr Teofil Blühbaum, whose nerves could no longer stand what was happening all around him, took 15g of Luminal (even one gram can be fatal). Less than half an hour later, his family found out and tried to save him. Although his stomach was pumped immediately, he was asleep for nearly four days solid; he only survived thanks to the doctors' exceptional efforts and immediate actions. He and his wife both survived the occupation, and moved to Szczecin after the war, where he changed his name to Murczyński and settled for good. Dr Czesław Murczyński served as vice-chancellor of the university there, before the Academy of Medicine was founded, and his wife worked at the clinic. The couple committed suicide in 1971. Both of them were extremely ill and partially paralysed. They left a note, in which they explained that after much consideration they had decided on this course of action, as they could not see any point in prolonging their difficult lives.

I know of a case where a female doctor who had elderly parents and an aged aunt decided at their insistence to cut short the ordeal of deportation by giving them potassium cyanide. She told me of her intentions the day before, and the following day she carried out her plan to the letter. After a last supper with wine, after the final embraces and farewells, when nobody could speak for tears, the three old people fell asleep forever. The daughter single-handedly carried their bodies to the hospital courtyard on Józefińska Street, where the corpses of those killed were laid.

I also knew a male doctor who, at the insistence of his gravely ill father, gave him an injection of potassium cyanide. Despite a large dose, he did not die immediately, as one would have expected, but he quickly lost consciousness; as it took over ten minutes for him to die, the poison had clearly lost its potency.

During the October deportation, a young SS man named Unterscharführer Horst Pilarzik made a bloody name for himself. His mere appearance in the street aroused mortal terror. People would keep to their houses, and even the OD men were reluctant to encounter him. His job was to shoot groups of Jewish workers on their way from work to the ghetto. He was the first person who dared to punch Spira in the face and to whip Gutter. It was later said that such actions appeased his criminal nature. During a conversation with several Jews at the Madritsch factory (where he would drop by every now and then), he told them, allegedly with a hint of remorse, that he could no longer bring himself to shoot people, that he just couldn't forgive himself for it, but this had been his first job since he left the special school he had attended in Germany. He said that never in his life had he seen so many Jews in one place as there were now in the ghetto, and that he had shot people without entirely realising what he was doing. His explanation was most peculiar.

Zgoda Square emptied at around five o'clock in the afternoon. The Germans left the ghetto, and the guards were taken off duty. This had been one of the cruellest and most tragic deportations. The workers who had left for their jobs that morning, leaving their loved ones in the ghetto, found it empty upon their return. The smashed front doors emanated the horror of what had just happened. The blood on the streets and in the entrance halls, the piles of corpses in the courtyards, and their relatives gone without a last farewell — all of this shattered what was left of their nerves. The weeping and wailing that evening exceeded anything I had previously experienced in the ghetto.

Some workers came back to their flats to find nervously scribbled farewell notes from their mothers or wives: "Don't worry about us, take care of yourself!"

People started looking for each other. A flame of hope flickered in the hearts of those who had been left behind in case perhaps their loved ones had hidden somewhere, perhaps they could still be found. They searched the attics and cellars, they called out names, telling them they could come out now because the Germans had gone. Unfortunately, there were very few people still in hiding. Relatives and friends fell into an embrace on sight, hugging each other tightly as they silently mourned those who had gone forever.

Then began attempts to save the lives of those who had been deported. Perhaps the train was still at the station? They didn't lose a single moment — they moved heaven and earth, trying to bribe the Germans, promising policemen, railwaymen and commissioners vast fortunes, any amount at all, just to save their loved ones. Telephone calls were made in all directions, and cars went out with heavily paid Germans. Even the German police were tempted to take part in these enterprises. They chased after trains which had always only just left the station and wouldn't be stopping at any others; beyond that supposedly the local authority came to an end, and nobody knew the destination of the trains. News about the route of the train would reach the ghetto — the direction in which it was heading was now known. Despite assurances from high-ranking Germans that this deportation would be the last, nobody believed anything or anyone.

I remember how, after the events of 28 October 1942, we found that Filip Schor was missing. We were very sad about it: we considered him lost, as he had been seen in one of the groups of deportees. So our joy was immense when at around nine o'clock in the evening the pharmacy door opened and Filip came bounding into the room. He was exhausted, he couldn't get a word out because of his asthma, but nevertheless sheer joy emanated from his sickly, weary face. Despite his severe asthma, by managing to slip away from the line in the dark, he had escaped from the clutches of death. After a short rest he recovered, laughed like a child, danced and sang. He had rarely been as happy in his entire life. "Well, if they couldn't get Filip today, they never will," he said with a hint of pride. And he was right — they never did get him. A few weeks later he fell seriously ill with pneumonia, and in a half-conscious state he dragged himself to the pharmacy. It was to be his last visit; a few days later he was dead. He died as a human being should, in his own bed. His wife and daughter were given permission to go to the cemetery, where he was brought in a horse-drawn hearse driven by a very kind gravedigger named Pinie Koza.

The October deportation claimed seven thousand victims who were taken away, and about six hundred more who were killed on the spot. The optimists' faith in surviving the war was severely shaken.

Late that night we were visited by Erwina Order-Panzer, an experienced nurse and Dr Fenigerowa's right hand at the gynaecological hospital. There was nobody in the ghetto who didn't know lovely Erwina. Always smiling and full of kindness to anyone in need, she was an exceptionally cheerful woman. She sat down on a stool and rested her weary head in one hand. As tears flowed from her eyes, she told us her story in a quiet, quivering voice. She had lost her beloved mother a few hours before. The Germans had taken her away with all the others in a goods train from Płaszów station, even though she could have saved herself. As she was walking along the street, which was full of people heading for Zgoda Square, she had heard cries for help coming from the window of a little house on Józefińska Street, so she had followed the voice. It turned out to belong to a young woman who was giving birth, and who was in no state to go outside. Erwina's mother decided to stay with the woman until the baby was born. When the Germans and the Jewish police carried out their searches a few hours later, they came upon the young woman in

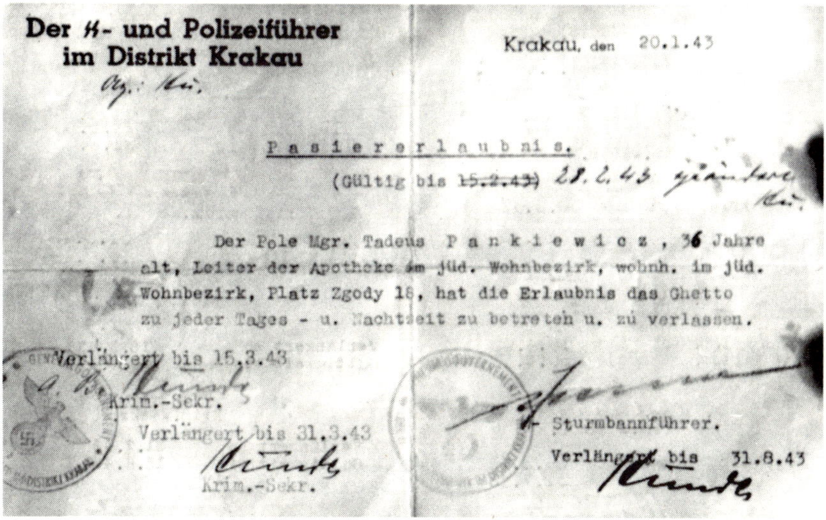
Der ß- und Polizeiführer
im Distrikt Krakau

Krakau, den 20.1.43

Pasiererlaubnis.

(Gültig bis ~~15.2.43~~) 28.2.43

Der Pole Mgr. Tadeus Pankiewicz, 36 Jahre alt, Leiter der Apotheke im jüd. Wohnbezirk, wohnh. im jüd. Wohnbezirk, Platz Zgody 18, hat die Erlaubnis das Ghetto zu jeder Tages - u. Nachtzeit zu betreten u. zu verlassen.

Verlängert bis 15.3.43

Krim.-Sekr.

Verlängert bis 31.3.43

Krim.-Sekr.

Sturmbannführer.

Verlängert bis 31.8.43

21. Tadeusz Pankiewicz's pass to enter
and leave the ghetto (1944)

labour and Erwina's mother. A curt order was issued: "Report for deportation immediately..."; at this point he pointed his whip at Erwina's mother, "...you, too". Erwina's mother tried to explain that she had the right to remain in the ghetto, that her daughter worked at the hospital, and that the families of health department employees were protected — but none of it helped. "*Raus, los, schnell!*" barked the German angrily.

People returning from work had no idea what had been happening in the ghetto in their absence. Anyone who went outside risked death. When Erwina found out what had happened to her mother, she took off her armband and, taking advantage of the confusion at the police station on the corner of Limanowski Street and Lwowska Street, she got out of the ghetto. In pursuit of her mother she raced like mad towards the station at Płaszów, from where the train full of deportees was due to depart. She reached the station and ran onto the platform where she saw various trains. She searched high and low, calling her mother's name, rushing from one train to the next...but unfortunately, the train she was looking for wasn't there, nobody knew anything and nobody could tell her anything. She returned to the ghetto, because her younger sister, sixteen-year-old Halinka, was there. She had also ended up on Zgoda Square among a group of deportees. I watched from the pharmacy window as an SS man pulled her from the crowd at the last minute and pointed her towards the exit. He had allowed her to live a little longer. She had rushed off in

22. Deportation of the children.
Drawing by A. Fenichel

the direction of Targowa Street. She survived the war: a split second of luck, a moment of good humour, and a mere whim had decided she should live.

Indeed, the Jews of Krakow perished without making any breaks for freedom, nothing on the scale of the fight to defend the Warsaw ghetto. But they died with dignity, with their heads held high, without demeaning themselves before their oppressors. With the exception of a small group of traitors, nearly everyone working at various enterprises carried out intentional, consistent sabotage. They did all they could to slow down the pace of work, to fail to meet deadlines, and to remove valuable items from the ghetto, or to destroy and burn them rather than have them fall into the hands of the Germans.

Active within the ghetto was a group known as the Jewish Combat Organisation (ŻOB), which cooperated with other resistance groups outside its walls. The following is a list of the heroes of this underground organisation, some of whom I knew personally: S. Dränger, Szymek M. Borowski and his wife Justyna, A. Liebeskind, Dolek Abe, Jan Ropa, Abraham Lejbowicz — "Romek Laban", a leading activist, Golda Mirer — the ŻOB's contact with the Polish resistance movement, Rajza Klingberg, Han-Balsamowich, Dawid Herz, Roman Bromberger, Moniek Eisenstein, Icchek Zuckerman, "Antek" — one of the leaders of the Warsaw ghetto uprising, Bauminger, Halbreich, and Warszawska.

This organisation's work involved many acts of sabotage against the German occupying forces.

In October 1942, members of the ŻOB set fire to several German lorries, trailers and fuel tanks situated at the army barracks on Grzegórzecka Street.

On 2 November 1942, they attempted to assassinate Gestapo informer Marcel Grüner and his wife, who had initially lived in the ghetto before moving to accommodation outside. That assassination attempt failed, but Grüner and his wife were killed later on, after the March deportations, sentenced to death by the secret organisation. One of the organisation's members, Robert Offner, was killed during that action. The successful assassination of a man named Adams from the General Government's Press and Propaganda Department was also the work of the ŻOB.

In September 1942, the ŻOB began printing a Polish-language magazine called *Głos demokratyczny* ("The Democratic Voice") which had a circulation of forty copies; approximately sixty issues of the magazine were published.

In October 1942, an assault division of the GL [*Gwardia Ludowa*] (People's Guard), which included the ŻOB "Iskra" organisation under the command of Jakub Halbreich, set fire to a garage on Włóczków Street housing three cars and some barrels of petrol.

Idek Libera was the leader of the "Iskra" organisation in December 1942. On 24 December 1942, they organised a bomb attack at the "Cyganeria" café on Szpitalna Street in Krakow. Eleven Germans were killed in the attack and thirteen were seriously wounded.

One of the leaders of the ŻOB in the Krakow ghetto, Adolf Liebeskind, was cornered by German police in one of the dives on Żuławski Street. A shootout ensued, during which Liebeskind killed two Germans and, seeing the hopelessness of his situation, used his revolver to take his own life.

One of the ŻOB rendezvous points was located outside the ghetto, at No.10 Skawińska Street. One day, German police officers entered the building suddenly and arrested everyone inside. Along with their leader, Abraham Leibowicz, they were taken to the camp at Płaszów, where they were later shot.

A name inextricably linked with the active conspirators was that of Szai Dreiblatt, a resident of the Krakow ghetto who from his first moment in the ghetto devoted all his spare time to constructing a bomb, with only a locksmith's workshop poorly equipped with the most primitive tools at his disposal. Of course, in these conditions he never managed to make a bomb, but his detailed plans for it were smuggled out of the ghetto, and became the basis for later production. In fact, it was a bomb of his design that went off at the "Cyganeria" café, mentioned above.

CHAPTER IV

THE CAMP AT PŁASZÓW — THE GHETTO IS MADE SMALLER AGAIN — EXECUTIONS AT PŁASZÓW — RELIABLE INFORMATION ABOUT THE FATE OF THE DEPORTEES — GHETTOS A & B — GHETTO RESIDENTS FROM OUTSIDE KRAKOW — AN ATTEMPT TO CLOSE THE PHARMACY — RESTRICTIONS — THE KINDERHEIM OPENS

It was after the October deportation that we first heard about plans to establish a camp on the site of the former Jewish cemetery in Płaszów. Each day dozens of Polish labourers were being hired to level the area. After a while, Jews were assigned to this work too. The more valuable gravestones, particularly those made of black marble, were dug up and set aside. Then they began bringing in timber for the construction of the barracks and equipment for installing a sewage system and for drilling a well. They fenced off the entire construction area with posts and barbed wire, and they built the watchtowers so typical of the Nazi concentration camps.

People were beginning to figure out for whom those barracks were intended. Yet again, the ghetto was flooded with rumours and speculation. The most "reliable" German sources gave assurances that they were for Poles, others claimed they were for Jews from France and Hungary, while others still said that all the young men from Krakow would be barracked there. However, the mixture of discouragement and indifference prevalent after the October deportation was plain to see.

In November 1942, we received quite definite news that the camp under construction in Płaszów was for the Jews of Krakow, that the ghetto's days were numbered, and its fate had been sealed. People were living in a state of anguish, and at the same time indifference. They began to ask in confusion: "What will happen to me?" "What about my loved ones?" "And what about the children?"

Some fell prey to deep neurosis, others were afflicted by chronic anxiety and racing thoughts, others were plunged into a state of mental apathy, incapable of considering or anticipating the near future.

"Mr Pankiewicz," said a regular visitor to the pharmacy, pointing towards the window overlooking Zgoda Square, "tell me why there are so few lunatics after everything people have gone through. Are those little grey cells in our brains really so immune to so much human misery? After all, there was no shortage of madmen before the war, but what did they suffer compared with our tragedies and misfortunes?"

After a pause, he spoke again.

"Tell me, what would happen if all of a sudden — today, say, at this very moment — the war were to end? Would all those people who regained their freedom go mad? I sometimes think about what would happen, and I really don't know. How lucky I am to be single, to have nobody in this world. And yet I am not indifferent to the people around me; I have become close to them, I have grown fond of their children, they have become part of my family. How strange it all is."

A flicker of hope for survival probably burned in the minds of everyone still safe so far, and the idea had not yet died that maybe one of his deported loved ones had miraculously remained alive and would return. My friend did survive the war, and paid me a visit.

"And yet I don't feel lucky, not in the full sense of the word," he said, lowering his voice.

As he shook my hand, he looked into my eyes for a long time and, as he was leaving, he said he would never forget me, but would write as soon as he settled down somewhere. He bid me farewell and left, but he never did write to me.

And in these conditions of loss and loneliness, time began to heal even the most painful wounds, and those who until recently had vowed never to get involved with anyone or start a family ever again began to look for new partners and enter into new marriages. Life is stronger than any resolution.

Even in the ghetto, immediately after their terrible experiences, those who were left alive sought partners to share their lives, and clandestine rabbis sanctioned these newly formed relationships.

At the Arbeitsamt, they updated the files and created new work assignments. They said that those employed at the same workplaces would soon be housed in particular blocks in the ghetto, so they wouldn't have to leave and return each day. It was becoming harder and harder to leave the ghetto to go to town. Obtaining a pass — even by offering a bribe — was more and more onerous, and people were afraid of one another, nobody trusted anybody else. Meanwhile, construction work at the camp in Płaszów progressed.

In November 1942, following the deportation, the ghetto was once again reduced in size. It was now becoming clear why the Germans had reversed their decision in October. Dąbrówka Street, Janowa Wola Street and the left side of Lwowska Street were removed from the ghetto.

Residents received a relocation deadline of twenty-four hours. And once again, eerie, terrifying scenes took place. The crowding was quite unimaginable. Several incompatible families were assigned a single room, which worsened the atmosphere, turned people into nervous wrecks and often drove them mad. There were constant arguments about the amount of things they had brought with them, about how much space they took up, about whose turn it was to light the kitchen stove, about how everyone would store their coal, and who had more or less of a right to be living there — this was the sad content of their everyday quarrels. For the first time people were allowed to move house throughout the night, and the ghetto was brightly illuminated from early evening onwards. The flurry of activity was tremendous. In both directions there were endless lines of people laden with everyday objects. While this was going on, Jewish workers erected a fence along the ghetto's new border. Again, no walls were built, just a series of posts with barbed wire stretched between them. This method of fencing off the ghetto confirmed speculation about its imminent liquidation.

Tenement buildings groaned under the weight of the accumulated furniture; a veritable labyrinth of wardrobes, dressers and bedside tables grew up in every courtyard, and porches and hallways swelled with trunks, boxes and antiques. Unsurprisingly, people's things kept disappearing — every day someone opened someone else's suitcase or broke into someone else's trunk. Coal disappeared here, bedlinen went missing there, elsewhere food. Existence was becoming horrendous, a real nightmare.

For people living together, co-existence became more and more difficult. Sometimes there were several families to every flat, and the communal kitchen became a hotbed of discord among the tenants. In moments of severe irritation, I heard things like: "Hitler knew how to take revenge on the Jews, and that's why he established this ghetto and crammed so many people into it". Heating a room shared by several people also proved to be a source of conflict. Nobody wanted to contribute to the purchase of coal, saying they were warm and there was no need to light the stove on their account. Such disputes drove people to the point of madness. I know of a case in which the occupants of one flat who — in their rage — refused to back down, opting instead to freeze all winter, even though the cellar was full of coal. Furniture also became a bone of contention. Everyone wanted to bring as much junk as they could to their new flats. But space was tight and there wasn't enough room for even part of the furniture. Whoever moved in first put in the most furniture, and those who came afterwards had to fight for a little bit of space, complaining and cursing all the while. Human pettiness and fondness for things manifest themselves even at life's most difficult times.

Kennkarten were declared invalid and the Jews had to use a *Judenpass* to prove their identities.

The ghetto was reduced in size by the set deadline and the moving was over. An enormous number of things had to be left where they were. Flats that had once belonged to deportees were sealed up, along with their entire contents. The German police and the Blue police went on duty in the deserted former ghetto streets.

Special labour units comprising Jews from the Arbeitsdienst began sorting through the household objects; furniture was taken out onto the street, where it was left to decay in the cold and rain for weeks on end. On 14 November 1942, the "Bulletin of Orders" carried a new order issued by the German authorities concerning the creation of five enclosed ghettos in the territory of the General Government: in Warsaw, Krakow, Lwów, Radom and Bełżec. All other areas were announced as being *judenrein*. The order instructed all Jews living outside the ghetto walls to return there. Some people were filled with a faint hope. And once again the Germans were victorious in their deceitful game, in the ingenious duplicity of their conduct. Many people returned to the ghetto, and the announcement discouraged many from leaving the ghetto; it made them drop their guard, only to take vengeance upon them all the more brutally later on.

And yet, in spite of all, life in the cramped ghetto continued in its strange and unnatural way. People's vitality was waning — though it was still there, perhaps manifesting itself in other ways. Each day groups of workers left the ghetto to work on the construction of the camp at Płaszów. Amon Göth, who would later succeed Müller as the camp's commandant, urged people to hurry up, constantly threatening to shoot them. As it later turned out, he was a man to be taken at his word, someone who regarded the murder and death of others as a trifle. He put pressure on the Judenrat and threatened to punish it for being slow to fulfil orders. Those who went out to work each day often did not return now; they were detained by the camp authorities and put in the barracks. These were the first forced inhabitants of Płaszów concentration camp.

One bleak day after the October operation, the appointed leader of the Judenrat, Dawid Gutter, and the head of the Ordnungsdienst, Symche Spira, were summoned to a conference at the SS und Polizeiführer headquarters on Oleandry Street. They came back late in the evening. The discussion must have been odd, because both men remained tight-lipped about the mysterious meeting. You could tell from their facial expressions that they hadn't heard anything good. And you could guess from their superficial comments that something was going to happen, but this time outside the ghetto. That night one of the Judenrat employees visited me at the pharmacy. And that's when I discovered what, among other things, was said at that conference on Oleandry Street: the following day, members of the Judenrat and the majority of the OD were to march from the ghetto towards Płaszów and there, next to the train station, they were to wait for the Gestapo. The most curious thing was that they were each told to bring talcum powder and a piece of rope of around a dozen metres in length. It wasn't hard to guess what for. There was going to be an execution, someone was going to be hanged; but the burning question was: who? There was also the possibility that it might even be someone, or several people from their own group. Everybody was nervous and nobody got any sleep that terrible night. People tried at all costs to dodge the order and remain in the ghetto. Doctors' certificates were supposed to excuse any absence, but very few people managed to get one.

The following morning, the Judenrat and Ordnungsdienst, lined up in fours, marched towards Płaszów, led by Spira and Gutter. Marching in front of them was an OD man named Feiler, an interesting character — a large, broad-shouldered man in his mid-forties who walked with a slight stoop. His beetroot-red face was that of a drunkard. Feiler was married but had no children, and he had come to the Krakow ghetto from the provinces. He didn't actually know how to talk, he just screamed (like the Germans) at everyone and everything.

He was always tipsy, but rarely ever drunk, despite the fact that he must have consumed a daily half litre of ninety-five percent spirit (which he found weaker by the day). He was an extremely simple man who was practically illiterate; apart from Yiddish, he spoke no other languages — his Polish was poor and his German even worse. Yet he was able to communicate effectively, the Germans understood him and he understood them. They took a shine to him because of his outward appearance, his ability to drink one glass of spirit after another, and the completely direct manner which he alone could get away with towards the Germans — he would pat an SS major or a Gestapo officer on the arm or leg, he could raise his hoarse voice at them, contradict them and express views contrary to theirs. Nothing ever happened to him, nobody ever hit him — he simply amused the Germans. By nature, Feiler was extremely nervous and over-excitable, and could quickly fly into a mad fit of rage for any reason, and it was quite remarkable the way his bloodshot eyes would almost pop out of their sockets. He screamed like a madman when this happened and he would hurl the most vulgar insults at his victims while beating them with his trusty cane. This was a man who was undoubtedly insane and yet unquestionably good. He was never in the service of the Germans. He didn't even want to remain in the ghetto after it was liquidated, but went instead to the camp in Płaszów with all the others, only returning to the ghetto each day with the workers. He was deeply and genuinely pained by the harm and misery done to his companions in misfortune and he cried like a baby after every execution — he was prepared to take risks and he pleaded for mercy for more than one person on several occasions. Many people owed their lives to him. Feiler was an OD man like the rest of them, just like Spira and his confederates, but he was also different from them in terms of the motives for and aims of his actions. The Germans liked him in spite of everything and they trusted him, but in a slightly different way from the other OD men. They never asked Feiler to spy or become an informer for them. He was able to maintain discipline and obedience, and he could carry out the Germans' orders without causing anybody personal harm. At the barracks in Płaszów he was put in charge of the warehouses full of Jewish property. His indirect superior was SS-Untersturmführer Popek. Feiler was supposedly shot and killed during an argument with a Ukrainian, but in fact Popek had shot him deliberately and with premeditation on the orders of higher authorities, probably because he was an inconvenient witness. An autopsy carried out by Dr F. Lewkowicz, a surgeon at the hospital in the Płaszów camp, established that the bullet was from a German revolver and not from the Ukrainian's rifle, as the Germans claimed. Yet this didn't prevent Balb from offering Feiler's wife his condolences upon the death of her husband. He promised that the perpetrator would be reprimanded and severely punished, and that she would be allowed to continue living in her flat outside the camp, in the barrack next to the warehouses. And yet nobody was at all surprised when less than a week later, Mrs Feiler was thrown out of the barrack and ordered to live in the main camp. And so this was the Feiler who led the Judenrat and Ordnungsdienst group to Płaszów, shouting orders at them to keep up.

That evening they all returned. This odd expedition was shrouded in mystery. However, the secret could not be kept for long and, despite the Germans' strict instructions not to tell anybody about their excursion, by evening the entire ghetto knew that the Gestapo had hanged prisoners brought there from Montelupich prison. The gallows had been set up right next to the railway tracks, and above them a sign stated that anyone who attempted to commit acts of sabotage would meet a similar fate. The Jews were forced to carry out the sentence. As for who those prisoners were, nobody knew. They were brought there in a tarpaulin covered truck. They had their hands tied behind their backs, and some of them looked Polish, some of them Jewish. Nobody was allowed to speak to them on pain of death. After listening to a speech about sabotage and the repressive measures which would be taken against anyone who committed similar acts, they set about carrying out the sentence. The prisoners were positioned on boards under the gallows. The Jews had to cut the ropes, put the nooses around the necks of the condemned men and, when given the order, pull the boards from under their feet. All of them were suspended above the ground at the same time. I received a detailed account of the execution that very evening from one of the participants in the expedition, an OD man named Rottersman. Rottersman was a good and honest man, and many Jews had a lot to thank him for. He told me that the Germans had photographed the entire spectacle in minute detail for propaganda purposes, to provide evidence of Jews murdering Poles. A similar execution took place a few weeks later.

After that first execution, many OD men became addicted to drink. They generally drank pure alcohol, and yet episodes of drunkenness were rare. People drank who had never known the taste of alcohol before; many of them sought relief and support in vodka as their nerves began to give way. Insomnia had become a widespread ailment too.

There was an extremely crafty fellow living in the ghetto called Oskar Feil, who coped perfectly well at all the tough moments. He always enjoyed telling us about his exploits. He took great pride in duping and playing tricks on the Germans. Feil offered his services as a expert at repairing typewriters and adding machines; he was initially employed by the Gestapo and later worked at the SS und Polizei office on Oleandry Street. While repairing the machines, he would say he needed all sorts of replacement parts, which he picked up from German warehouses filled with typewriters stolen from the Poles and Jews. He was guarded by a German policeman when he made these visits. On site, he would take the best parts from new machines and then make his way (under escort) to a machinery workshop on Floriańska Street, which was owned by Polak Młodecki. Młodecki knew the situation, and paid Feil in cash for these parts; he then gave Feil some old scrap metal, which Feil later threw away. In Młodecki's workshop they were allegedly making some minor alterations. And all of this took place right in front of the German policeman! In this way, Feil was able to sell several new typewriters and an adding machine. And here is another of his little stunts. During the time when the so-called Blauscheine were being issued, when people stood in queues for days on end in the extreme heat, unsure of whether they would get this document or not (which was tantamount to deportation), after a little thought, Feil took a ladder which was standing nearby, pushed his way through the crowd and entered the council building. Inside, he calmly climbed up the ladder and began to fiddle with an electrical socket; incidentally, he didn't know the first thing about electrics. After a while he came down the ladder and, holding it under one arm, handed one of the Germans his Kennkarte; the German automatically issued him with the required blue card.

And then in Płaszów there was Henryk Goldschmidt, a graphic artist by trade, who, like Feil, was escorted to the SS und Polizei office each day, where on a large wall he wrote out the following slogan in Gothic lettering: *Es ist gänzlich unwichtig, ob wir leben, aber wichtig ist, dass unser Volk, dass Deutschland lebt* ("It is entirely unimportant whether we live, but it is important that our people, that Germany lives"). He worked away at this nonsense quietly and happily for several weeks, until some policeman-cum-philosopher had a brainwave that it was inappropriate for a Jew to be writing such solemn aphorisms; and so his slogan writing was brought to an end.

In November 1942, a letter arrived in the ghetto from a relative of one of the doctors, who had escaped just before the October deportation and gone to Lwów. On her way there she had passed through Bełżec. I held that letter in my hands, and my colleagues and I read it. The content of the letter spread like wildfire through the entire ghetto. After all the rumours, it was — you could say — the first genuine confirmation of what was being said in all sorts of versions about the fate of the deportees. Its author gave a realistic description of the trains full of people that stopped at Bełżec, often waiting there for days on end for their destiny, which meant to be driven onto side-tracks into a dense forest surrounded by a barbed wire fence. Thick smoke trailed over the forest non-stop, and an uncanny, nauseating smell lingered in the air. The people living in Bełżec said that the deportees who had survived the horrors of the journey in closed goods trucks sometimes had to stand at the station for several days without a drop to drink or a bite to eat. They heard the deportees' moans and pleas, but weren't allowed to help. The Germans were guarding each train. Once a train entered the forest, the guards opened the truck doors, and those who were still alive were ordered to strip naked and then forced into gas chambers. Their bodies were then cremated, and that was the source of the constant smoke that hung over the forest. At the end of the letter, the writer appealed to people to stop deluding themselves about the fate of the deportees; anyone who could, should escape as soon as possible, before it was too late. This news made a terrible impression in the ghetto and dispelled the last remains of people's illusions.

News began to spread once more that there was to be another deportation. It was said that Zgoda Square was to be cut off from the ghetto. And again, people began pinning their hopes on this news: if Zgoda Square were cut off, there would be nowhere to carry out deportations, so they would probably stop. The authorities' announcement about the creation of five permanent ghettos within the General Government confirmed this speculation. Considering their extraordinary living conditions and countless horrific experiences, no wonder people drew such far-reaching and almost always erroneous conclusions from mere tidbits of information.

At the beginning of December 1942, engineers appeared on Targowa Street and Zgoda Square. With plans in their hands, they demarcated borders and took some measurements. The ghetto was apparently going to be divided, but nobody knew anything definite. A few days later we found out that the ghetto would be divided into two parts. Trucks brought in posts and barbed wire. Judenrat members Salomonowicz and Günter had determined the borders for the two areas.

On 6 December, the ghetto was divided into two parts: ghetto A and ghetto B. Following this, a new order was issued: all workers living in ghetto B had to move to ghetto A and, conversely, all non-workers from ghetto A were to move to ghetto B. The dividing line ran right in front of my pharmacy, which ended up in ghetto B, to which those living in ghetto A were to have no access.

Once again the moving began, the search for new flats, and efforts to carry one's remaining belongings on one's back. Almost nobody took items of furniture with them this time; instead, they generally destroyed them, smashing them up by throwing them from balconies and windows onto the courtyards below, and then setting fire to them. From early morning, the noise of falling wardrobes, sideboards, tables and stools echoed around the courtyards. With each passing day, ghetto B began to empty, whereas ghetto A became more and more packed. About a fortnight later, they closed the passage between ghettos A and B. The gate separating the two districts was closely guarded by OD men. To get from ghetto A to the pharmacy, you needed to obtain a pass from the OD. Initially, this was fairly easy but, as time went on, they made it more and more difficult, until finally they introduced an outright ban. This meant that people living in ghetto A were completely cut off from the pharmacy. Hardly anyone came to see us — the inhabitants of ghetto B were all unemployed, generally poor people with nothing to live on. To solve the problem of obtaining medical supplies, the OD operated a pharmacy service, running back and forward between us and the people waiting beyond the barbed wire fence opposite. It was a complete mess. These people were unqualified and they would mix up prescriptions (especially when it was dark), swap the drugs around and give the wrong names of medicines — it was sheer madness. On SS orders the OD was replaced by a worker — a young office boy from the Judenrat. The German authorities gave orders for him to wear a hat labelled *Apotheke*. From then on, this boy acted as middleman between us and our customers, and he was paid for this work by both the pharmacy and the Judenrat. The boy was very smart and, as he was a quick learner, there were no more mistakes. He was well-liked by everyone because he was polite and always smiling so that in time, issuing medicines through the barbed wire no longer caused the customers any problems — but we must have been the only pharmacy in the world which only had one customer come through its doors for a period of several months. The *Apotheke* hat worn by that young lad would have made a unique exhibit at the Polish Pharmaceutical Museum. On 13 March 1943, the day the ghetto was liquidated, this anomaly came to an end too.

Jews from small neighbouring towns were brought to ghetto B. They were a shabby lot, half-starved and barefooted, covered in lice and unshaven for several months. Their terror-filled eyes stared vacantly into space.

They occupied empty flats and deserted buildings. Most of them had never been outside the village where they were born and they had never seen a large city in their lives before. I don't think they even knew what was happening around them, if they even realised there was a war going on, or about the existence of Hitler, the SS and the Gestapo. Some of them were imbeciles, at least many of those who lived in the same building as the pharmacy were. I tried to approach them to find out more about them, but they were like bears trapped in a cage, endlessly walking the length of the barbed wire fence and begging the passers-by in ghetto A for a piece of bread. They had brought literally nothing with them; their only possessions were the dubious contents of their tattered pockets. Many of them were barefooted, but it was the middle of winter, there was frost on the ground, it was cold indoors and the water in the pipes was generally frozen. These people slept on the floor — the lucky ones found a little straw or hay to sleep on. Their fingers and toes were frostbitten, their bodies were covered in sores, scurvy was endemic, as were scabies and other skin diseases.

We helped them as much as we could. We attended to their sores and frostbitten extremities, we shared our bread with them and we gave them hot tea fortified with a little alcohol. For us, their every smile was gratitude enough. The OD prohibited them from leaving their homes. But their hunger was stronger than any prohibition or threats. Unable to cope with them, the OD nailed up the doors and windows of their buildings so nobody could get outside. Once, sometimes twice a day, the OD fed them like wild animals in cages. They lunged for the food and swallowed whole chunks without chewing; a second later, there wasn't a single crumb left.

They burnt anything made of wood. In the building which housed the pharmacy, all the wardrobes, tables and chairs vanished into thin air. Within a few weeks, they had burnt the banisters, the stairs to the cellar, doors from empty flats, window frames, and they even tore up floorboards. Reaching the attic or the basement at that time was simply impossible. To make matters worse, the water pipes burst and water streamed down the walls and flooded the rooms. There was nothing anyone could do because nobody was allowed to enter ghetto B. In the end I was able to obtain permission for a plumber to come in to turn the water off. The pharmacy was without water — I needn't describe what state the toilets were in; several hundred people were shut inside the building and there was no water. By the time the ghetto was vacated, huge piles of human waste a metre high and several metres in length had accumulated in front of the entrance to the toilets in the courtyard. From time to time, sometimes even twice a day, OD men would assemble people in the courtyard and get them to list their names and occupations; the OD men wrote everything down on special forms. In an effort to save themselves, some people passed themselves off as master craftsmen, even though they didn't have a clue about the given trade.

It was 1943. The winter was harsh, as were the conditions in the ghetto. People were counting the weeks until they would have to leave their homes in the brick tenement buildings, say goodbye to their possessions and furniture, and move to wooden barracks in the windswept heights of the Płaszów cemetery. But that wasn't the most important thing. What would happen to the children? How would this resettlement be done? Would everyone go? These questions preoccupied everybody's minds and gave them sleepless nights.

The Arbeitsamt divided the working population of ghetto A into three categories, each of them marked by a letter: R (*Rüstung*), W (*Wehrmacht*) and Z (*Zivil*). These letters were written on a square of cloth, impressed with an SS und Polizei stamp, and then sewn onto the left-hand side of the jacket, at chest level. This was a compulsory addition to the Judenpass. The SS und Polizei now assumed the role previously performed by the Arbeitsamt. From now on, the SS und Polizei would be the authority responsible for referring Jewish workers, or dismissing them from their current jobs.

The camp at Płaszów was growing. People said special children's barracks were being built there and that there would even be a kindergarten. It was said there would be shops there, that the character of the ghetto wouldn't change, that there would be no more deportations, and that there would be enough room for everyone there. No prizes for guessing who the author of those rumours was, or who was counting on people dropping their guard.

There *were* people, though not many, who believed these rumours.

And so the seemingly normal life of the ghetto continued. Life was not peaceful, however. Trucks arrived almost daily, and SS men carried out round-ups: they dispersed through the streets and grabbed people, punching and kicking them, regardless of whether they were young or old, or whether they worked or not. The streets would empty at the sight of those trucks; people hid in their homes, waiting several hours before they ventured out again.

At the pharmacy, every single room was full of friends, especially in the back rooms, whence it was easy to escape through the exit. It is hard to take in the fact that people managed to do it, and that we all had good fortune in that critical situation. The attics and cellars were full of escapees too. But where were the informers then?

Amid the shocking impressions afforded by resettlement, constant round-ups, nightly arrests, and people being sent off to concentration camps, one day followed the next. In the pharmacy, we were visited by a stream of friends — they always found a way to reach us. Every day brought new discussion, whether about Hans Frank's latest speeches, or the most recent war communiqués; from these they developed theories and tried to calculate their chances of survival. They came to the conclusion that some Jews would survive, and that the Germans couldn't possibly murder them all. As if remembering a charming fairy tale, people would sigh with relief at the thought of the day they would be liberated, when the Germans would flee. That was all they were waiting for, just to see the Germans' defeat. Even the desire for revenge was put into the background. The underground press lifted everybody's spirits. Another distributor of the underground newspapers who visited us at the pharmacy was a man named Antoni Krawczyk, whose son was executed in front of the synagogue on Szeroka Street.

In January 1943, the one and only fire broke out in the ghetto: a shop selling paint and turpentine on Limanowski Street went up in flames. A woman jumped out of a window on the first floor, but then the fire brigade arrived and put out the fire.

On 15 January 1943, as I was returning to the ghetto after dinner, I found out from an OD man standing at the gate that the chief of the German police, Bousko, had asked me to report to him immediately. I went there and Bousko told me that Sturmbannführer Haase from the SS und Polizei had just been to the ghetto, and had given orders for the pharmacy to be closed and for nobody to be allowed in. I was horrified and asked Bousko for advice. There was only one way out: Haase might change his mind.

"The only option you have," said Bousko, "is to go and see Haase at Oleandry Street first thing tomorrow and raise the matter with him."

At that moment I knew my situation was hopeless. I knew that getting Haase to change his mind was impossible. And yet I decided to try my luck.

The following day I went to see the authorities at the Department of Health. The German officials in the *Gesundheitswesen*[1] were relatively obliging towards the pharmacists of Krakow; moreover, it was easy to come to an arrangement with them in the traditional manner. The value of the arguments usually used by petitioners in support of their case was not too great. A bottle of perfume, the biggest size of nylon stockings, a bottle of vodka, a box of cigars — and then you could come to an understanding. And so it happened. Armed with these "arguments", I presented my case and was given the necessary papers for the SS und Polizeiführer. I now had it in black and white — the closure of the pharmacy would have a detrimental effect on the health of the ghetto residents, and if the Jews were denied medicine, the ghetto would become a hotbed of disease and epidemics which not even the ghetto walls or barbed wire could contain. The next day, I ventured into the lion's den. I reported to see Haase and then sat in the waiting room. The door to Haase's office opened and there, in all his glory, stood the man who had murdered thousands of people. In a dry voice, he announced that all matters pertaining to the ghetto could only be taken care of by Kunde, his officer for Jewish Affairs. But Kunde wasn't there.

The next day I went back to Haase's office where I chanced upon Kunde, whom I knew very well from

1 *Gesundheitswesen* (Ger.) The Health Service.

the ghetto. I gave him my documents and briefly told him about my request. He took me into his office, asked me to take a seat and then offered me a cigar.

The conversation began. Kunde regretted the war and its countless victims, but blamed our pre-war government for it all. He told me that, as a father of two children, as a husband, he hated being separated from his family — he even showed me photographs of his parents, wife and children. He talked about his homesickness and about the beauty of Krakow, and said that he would like to live in Krakow when the war was over. He claimed that like every German he was disgusted by *Volksdeutsche*[1], and about how *they* were the biggest pigs, each of them holding onto as many posts as they could, and changing their allegiance whichever way the wind was blowing. He expressed his fondness for the Poles, adding that he was sure many of them would gladly become *Reichsdeutsche*[2] — if that were at all possible — but not *Volksdeutsche*. He could not understand the political views of certain individuals who wanted to regard the Poles as inferior, because he only divided people into two categories: decent and not decent. He

1 *Volksdeutsche* (Ger.) (lit. "ethnic Germans") was the term used to describe citizens of Nazi-occupied territories (i.e. outside the German Empire) who were officially registered as ethnic Germans.

2 *Reichsdeutsche* (Ger.) (lit. "Imperial Germans") referred to the ethnic citizens of the German Reich.

talked about everything except my ghetto passes. After this dialogue — or rather *monologue*, given that he did all the talking and I simply listened in bewilderment — we finally got down to business. He read through my documents from the Gesundheitswesen and asked me a few questions and, among other things, after trying to convince me that my surname wasn't Polish, he filled out forms that would allow me and my staff to enter and exit the ghetto at any time of day or night. They still required Haase's signature. I waited for a while. Unfortunately, Haase didn't sign the passes because, due to the strict new rules regarding the complete isolation of the Jews from the Aryans, the passes could only be issued if they had a guarantor, which in my case would be the Gesundheitswesen. I left the office without really knowing what they meant. How could Germans act as guarantors for a Pole? Even the Gesundheitswesen didn't understand what the SS had in mind. They made lengthy telephone calls and spoke to several officers — in the meantime, I ran around town buying gifts. Finally, the letter was ready. I attached a guarantee of my own, on behalf of myself and my staff, in which I vowed that I would not come into contact with the Jews, that our conversations would be strictly limited to the issuing of medicines, that I would not bring German or Polish newspapers into the ghetto, and that I would not discuss political matters or assist the Jews in any way whatsoever.

I spent the next day waiting for Kunde. I waited from eight in the morning until noon. He arrived and was just as polite as he had been the previous day. I gave him the annexes and waited for the result. A few minutes later I was given signed passes, valid for fifteen days. I took a risk and tried to give him a bottle of vodka. He didn't take it, but said he would drop in at the pharmacy when he was next in the area. From then on, he began to visit us several times a day.

My duty room was witness to many interesting and clandestine visits, because Kunde conducted meetings with certain individuals there. He didn't want to take these people to his own office, which was located in the same building as the Jewish police. How many mysterious characters and informers from towns all over the Krakow district passed through that room! Almost every one of them wore dark glasses and they all spoke German fluently. None of them wore armbands. They spoke in hushed voices, so we couldn't hear a word on the other side of the door. Each session generally lasted about half an hour. It was never the case for two people to arrive together, and they were so punctual that literally two minutes after one person had left, the next one appeared.

One time — I remember it was a hot, sunny Saturday — I went outside the pharmacy and saw, much to my surprise, a slender young woman clad entirely in black coming in through the guardroom gate. She had a black veil covering half her face, and no armband. At a slow pace she approached the pharmacy. She came inside, lifted her veil and asked me if I was the owner. "Yes, that's me," I replied. She slowly removed a long black glove and then offered me her hand as she introduced herself: "Ronikerowa. Kunde has authorised me to wait for him here". I led her into the duty room and she sat down. I offered her a coffee and she accepted. A few minutes later, Kunde arrived, and there was a perfunctory exchange of views. I slowly withdrew from the room but didn't close the door fully behind me. The discussion became more and more animated, and her voice became louder and louder. Kunde spoke quietly and calmly. I managed to catch the odd word. It was about intervening for someone who had been arrested. Several times Dr Kazimierz Piotrowski's name was mentioned. Piotrowski was an extremely well-known doctor in Krakow, a much sought-after gynaecologist; he was also a theatre critic and had an impressive knowledge of various subjects. The conversation probably concerned one of the doctor's close relatives. The mysterious woman reproached Kunde: "If you're working on it, then why haven't you kept your word? This matter was supposed to have been sorted out ages ago". Kunde defended himself and his colleagues. An hour later, after drinking black coffee and several glasses of vodka, the conversation ended and they left. She said goodbye to me and thanked me for my hospitality.

An unusual event took place in that room, something one could call "black humour". One afternoon, Kunde came into the room, holding three pairs of handcuffs.

"Guess what," he said, "we're going to play a little joke on the ladies in the pharmacy."

"What kind of joke?"

"I'll handcuff you, and then we'll walk out of the pharmacy together, making sure the ladies see us. We'll go over there," he said, pointing through the window towards the corner of the building facing the pharmacy. "We'll hide from view there and I'll fire my revolver. Then I'll remove the handcuffs and we'll come back. The girls will think I've shot you, it'll be a real hoot," he said.

"What a sick joke," I thought as he handcuffed me. After a while we got up and left. My pharmacy ladies looked on, dumbstruck with terror and not understanding a thing. We went and stood round the corner of the building opposite. Kunde pulled out his revolver and I commended my soul to God, not knowing for certain what was about to happen. He fired a shot in the air, put his gun back in its holster and then took the handcuffs off. Laughing, we emerged from the side street. I must admit that I didn't really feel like laughing. And I can't describe what must have been happening in the pharmacy at that time. My ladies were sure I'd been shot. But at least the grim joke had a happy ending.

The year 1943 didn't begin so merrily. In accordance with recently issued orders from Berlin concerning the strict segregation of Jews from the Aryan population, a new order came into force in the ghetto which prohibited Jews from using streets which bordered the Aryan side and were separated from it by barbed wire.

All shops on those streets were to be automatically closed down, unless they had an entrance from the courtyards at the rear. Traffic on those streets came to a complete stop. Shops and entrances were locked. Only the occasional OD man would walk along the empty pavements. The ghetto was closed, and now it was entirely concealed from outsiders, jealously guarding its hidden secrets from the world. Inside the ghetto, an order was posted which summoned Jews to the barracks at Płaszów. The commandant of the future camp was insisting the deportation be carried out as quickly as possible, and setting the Judenrat new tasks which were difficult — or utterly impossible — to implement. For example, he ordered the disinfection unit on Józefińska Street to deal with three hundred people a day, i.e. to wash them, shave off their hair and disinfect them. The manager of the unit, a pharmacist named Raschbaum, told me the SS had accused him of sabotaging German orders because the unit was functioning too slowly. With a pencil in his hand, he demonstrated to the Germans that what they were expecting was physically impossible; their response was that those numbers were to be increased by fifty percent, and that if he didn't do it, he'd be shot.

The Gestapo was actually reluctant to agree to close down the ghetto, and they attempted to delay the matter at every turn. Abolishing the ghetto and relocating the entire Jewish population to the barracks at Płaszów would deprive many of them of lucrative business within the General Government, and there was even a danger of being sent to the front.

The camp in Płaszów was beginning to fill up. Its first inhabitants were joiners, bricklayers, locksmiths and everyone else who was employed in the construction of the barracks. The Germans made daily announcements listing which workers were to be deloused and sent to the barracks; they were told they could take as many items as they could carry. The liquidation of the ghetto was becoming a reality. It was only a matter of time before this tragedy reached its final act, and by what means it would happen.

On German orders, a *Kinderheim* — or children's home — was opened in the ghetto. Gutter and Spira attended the opening. It was quite a ceremony: there were new lies and new deceit, and once again people dropped their guard. Parents who were working could bring in children up to the age of fourteen. There, supervised by experienced carers, the children were kept busy with various tasks, such as sealing envelopes and weaving baskets. They were also taught how to sew, so that they could help the adults at the *Gemeinschaften*[I] once the ghetto was moved to the camp. Each day the Kinderheim was filled by dozens of children, who eagerly and happily ran there, naively unaware of the great dangers and tragedy which loomed over them. And to think

I *Gemeinschaft* (Ger.) ("community"), here: a crafts association.

that all this was implemented a few weeks before the pre-determined murder of every child in the Kinderheim. But the children happily worked away, while their parents were glad at their willingness to work and the progress they were making.

CHAPTER V

TRANSPORTS TO THE CAMP AT PŁASZÓW — THE LIQUIDATION OF THE GHETTO, 13–14 MARCH 1943 — PSYCHOLOGICAL RIDDLES — THE MURDER OF PATIENTS AND CHILDREN — NIGHTMARISH SCENES

And so the days went by, all alike in their hopelessness and all full of the blackest predictions for the future. The population of the ghetto was getting smaller from one day to the next — transports left for the camp at Płaszów nearly every day. In the first few weeks there was no visible change, because even so, in relation to the number of buildings in the ghetto the number of people crowded together was enormous.

As well as the people working on the barracks at Płaszów, the camp now housed those employed at many other factories and workshops outside the ghetto too, such as the "*Emailwarenfabrik*", Krakow airport, Kabel, the workshops at Montelupich, the *Zentrale für Handwerkslieferungen*, Juliusz Madritsch's clothing factory (at No.2 Podgórski Market Square), the *Deutsche Rüstungsfabrik* in Zabłocie (a suburb of Krakow), the barrack factory in Zabłocie, the brickyard in Bonarka (another suburb), the military vehicles plant, the Gestapo's technical workshop on Pomorska Street, at Wawel Castle (Wawel-Burg), and the City Cleansing Works. Only at some of these workplaces were the Jews kept in on-site barracks. At the rest, the Jewish workers were brought in each day under heavy guard, and escorted back to the

Płaszów camp after work. Long columns of haggard and emaciated people — the victims of physical and mental abuse — were seen walking slowly through the streets of the former ghetto; how much sadness and pain there was in their lifeless eyes. How great their feelings of disgust and contempt must have been towards the Nazis who had dreamt up all those forms of harassment. "It's you today, but tomorrow it could be us" — that's the thought which must have occurred to every rational being as his eyes passed along those rows of people, more like ghosts than the living, in search of one of his friends or relatives. At that time all of us — those of us living outside the camp and those who were at so-called liberty — were alarmed on a daily basis by new events and experiences, which all shared the same content and the same name: beating, arrest and death.

The first transports left for the Julags[1] — small camps at Płaszów, Prokocim and Bonarka.

The first doctor to move from the Krakow ghetto to the Płaszów concentration camp was Dr Leon Gross. He was to become the camp's chief medical officer, simply because he was the first doctor to have arrived there. Meanwhile, the Judenrat kept putting off having to go "up the hill" to the barracks. Down here it was more or less possible to survive — but "the hill" filled people with sheer terror. In this period, many OD men left

1 *Jüdischelager* (Ger.), Jewish camps.

23. Sections of the ghetto wall on Lwowska Street

the ghetto to take up various posts at the camp. Other residents offered to take their place, because the demand for OD men was still great, and there was a hope of saving oneself and one's family this way. Spira himself was responsible for hiring or rejecting candidates. Each candidate was given an exam: he had to stand to attention two metres in front of Spira, salute him, and in a loud, firm voice state his name and duties, and declare that he was at the boss's disposal. This report had to be done in Polish and in German. And that was the entire exam. Selection depended on the candidate's appearance, whether or not he had friends in high places, and Spira's mood that day.

With liquidation looming, there was growing anxiety in the ghetto. Each day somebody left. People said goodbye to each other forever, and left their homes taking only the small, valuable objects with them. At the OD building, German officers for Jewish Affairs were spending long days filling out mountains of forms, writing reports and typing up reports of prisoner interrogations from the ghetto prison. Somebody escaped from the ghetto almost every day. The shops were gradually disappearing: they were not stocking up any more, and the supplies they had were quickly running out. People were literally living from one day to the next, spending whatever they earned. For several days, the Judenrat, led by Gutter, had been attempting to push back the deadline for the liquidation of the ghetto at any cost, but all their attempts failed. Haase wouldn't extend

24. The "Pod Orłem" pharmacy building (taken in 1982), currently the Museum of National Remembrance at the "Pod Orłem" Pharmacy

the deadline even by a day. On 13 March 1943, at 11 am, on the orders of SS-Obergruppenführer Scherner, the Judenrat told the inhabitants of ghetto A they had until 3 pm to march to the camp in Płaszów. The following day, the inhabitants of ghetto B were to be sent to Ostbahn workplaces. The Sonderdienst — comprising Latvians, Lithuanians, Ukrainians and members of the Blue Police — surrounded the ghetto; a small number of police guards entered the ghetto and positioned themselves along the length of passage connecting ghetto A to ghetto B. You could pass from ghetto A to ghetto B with no trouble at all, but not in the opposite direction.

The mood was awful and the scenes were indescribable. People rushed anxiously from street to street, screaming to one another. Laden with belongings, they ran around looking for co-workers and loved ones. There were about a dozen Germans circulating within the ghetto, led by Amon Göth, who was driving people along the streets, holding a sub-machine gun. The presence of Göth and his entourage (which included his ever-present dogs, Ralf and Rolf) compounded everybody's anxiety. The OD men were running around like madmen. They began liquidating the hospitals.

Watching from the pharmacy window, I saw the commotion suddenly stop. Nobody screamed, nobody called out — there was deathly silence. Everyone stood and stared in the direction of Targowa Street. "Someone must be coming along that street, someone terrifying," I thought. And sure enough, Amon Göth appeared, a tall, handsome man with blue eyes, about forty years of age, with a well-proportioned head, a large body and skinny legs. He was dressed in a long black leather coat, with his two enormous dogs at his side; in one hand he held a riding crop and in the other an automatic rifle. The OD men stiffened to attention in front of him. Seemingly oblivious to the presence of others, he walked across Zgoda Square before disappearing up Solna Street. People heaved a sigh of relief and then rushed towards the entrance gate. Dignitaries drove into the ghetto to intervene on behalf of their own people and to ensure they were able to leave. I saw one car belonging to Heinemayer, the head of the Gestapo's political branch, and another belonging to his deputy, Sipo officer Körner. Those they defended left the ghetto in the Germans' cars. Marcel Grüner and his wife (whom I mentioned earlier) left in a furniture van loaded with all their personal belongings. Körner got two doctors out, who, it was later said, escaped to Warsaw and from there to Hungary. All of this took place before our very eyes.

The Germans were masterful at generating an atmosphere of panic, threat and fear. The noise of gunshots, whistles, dogs barking and Germans screaming was a strangely unpleasant mixture. Fear for the lives of their children was depriving people of their reason. Some hid their children under beds, in wardrobes, and in other hiding places. Some of the children wandered around the streets, asking strangers for help — to no avail. Their parents had no idea what to do. It was almost time to leave and they weren't allowed to take minors with them. In the group that was ready to leave stood husbands and wives waiting for their spouses, and adult children waiting for their parents. The Germans kept assuring people that all the minors would be going to the camp, but later on, after the adults — as they knew, a special children's barrack was being built.

As doctors left the hospitals, they informed their patients of the Germans' orders for everyone to remain in their beds. However, they explicitly told them what would happen to them if they stayed in the hospital. "Those of you who can — save yourselves," they said. Patients began fleeing in panic. Anyone who was capable of standing upright left the hospital — post-operative patients, old and young, convalescent and in a fever. I saw seriously ill patients from the hospital for infectious diseases in the alley next to Zgoda Square running in all directions, in their nightclothes (or half-naked). It was an incredible scene. People gathered their remaining strength, but they kept falling over and hurting themselves, then getting up and dragging themselves onwards; others were assisted by family members. Nobody knew what to do with the ones who couldn't bear their own weight, and who, as they were passing through the main gate, would have to hold on tight so that nobody would notice they were sick. However, not everybody was capable of escaping from the hospital, some people were just too weak to get out of bed; those people stayed behind, knowing perfectly well what awaited them. A last goodbye, a last squeeze of the hand from a friend or neighbour leaving the hospital, a last request or instruction for their loved ones, and then a deathly silence filled the deserted rooms.

In the ghetto, people rushed around feverishly and ran in all directions. Anyone who could do so hid and protected their most valuable objects. We delivered our friends' things to a number of addresses in town. It wasn't possible to hide many things in the pharmacy, as we were at risk of being searched at any time. Empty drawers in the pharmacy were used as a temporary repository for all sorts of objects — some were valuable, others were worthless but had sentimental value for their owners. Nobody demanded a receipt, nobody was overly concerned about how their things would be stored. All that mattered was the keeper's honesty. People were hoping to sell their deposited items later on, and use the money to survive their time in the barracks. This allowed many people to survive terrible periods of starvation. We sent various parcels and letters to them from the pharmacy via Dr Michał Weichert, the head of the Jewish organisation for Social Aid (JUS), which delivered medicines and food to Jews at Płaszów concentration camp, and to many other places outside Krakow. The people we assisted trusted us implicitly. The ladies working at the pharmacy risked their lives to meet the requests of those who went to Płaszów.

However, not everybody who received objects for safekeeping returned them at their owners' request.

More than once, to our embarrassment, we had to inform prisoners in the barracks from whom we had received instructions to fetch items being kept for them that they were gone, because they had been confiscated during a search, or because the people keeping the items would only return them to their owners in person — which everyone knew was impossible, because no one was allowed to leave the camp. They would refuse to give us the items, despite receiving handwritten letters from their owners, though they knew the sender's handwriting as well as the password they had agreed upon when they took the objects for safe-keeping.

Yet there were many honest people who gave back everything entrusted to them, and who looked after them as if they were their own. And there were even those who would often provide help out of their own resources.

The moment of resettlement was fast approaching. With bundles in their hands, people were put into tightly-packed groups of four, all ready to depart, just waiting for the order. By now everyone wanted to be "up the hill"; they had had enough of this endless uncertainty. Almost all of them thought the barracks at Płaszów would be the last leg of their journey, the final stage in their nomadic, insecure existence. The camp sounded decidedly permanent to these poor wretches: there probably wouldn't be any more deportations — if you survived this, you would go on living. That was the general opinion.

Unfortunately, there was something extremely alarming about this final act in the liquidation of the Krakow ghetto, which was the fate of the children. The matter still hadn't been settled, it was up in the air, and thus a source of great anxiety. At the Judenrat, the Germans held endless discussions, the upshot of which was that the Germans gave orders and the Jews had to carry out their instructions. The Judenrat members left the building, with the Gestapo officers and SS men ahead of them. In a flash, the terrible news spread through the assembled crowd: they were not allowed to take their children with them. All children under fifteen were to stay behind. Parents were stunned by the news: this was something new, this was something they hadn't bargained on. And yet it had happened during all previous deportations, and had been an unremitting tragedy for anyone with young children. Time and again people were fooled, and time and again they suffered painful disappointment. And so it was this time too. They had believed in those specially-built children's barracks, they had believed in the usefulness of the recently opened Kinderheim, they had believed the Germans' solemn promises that all parents and children would be together in the barracks up the hill. Now too, the Germans had not yet broken their promise, they had just moved the deadline. The younger children wouldn't go right now, but would be brought in trucks once the adults had moved across. They were told to leave their children at the Kinderheim. And this time too, some of the people believed them.

However, many mothers did not trust the Germans, and did not believe their assurances. They refused to leave their children on their own, so they left their groups and went to ghetto B, which had another twenty-four hours of existence ahead of it. Husbands yielded to their wives' persuasion and stayed behind in the groups; fooled into thinking they'd be able to do something for their loved ones, they believed in a miracle. The women who stayed behind were nameless and noble heroines, making a silent sacrifice. These scenes left an unforgettable impression on everyone who witnessed them. Total strangers wept as they saw the pain and helplessness of those who remained. This was a hundred times more terrifying than any physical bullying, or even the killing of defenceless people. Wandering children were taken by force to the Kinderheim, which was now packed full.

There were nightmare scenes at the pharmacy. People were numb with pain, totally crushed. Friend after friend came in to tell us that their husband or wife was in the queue to leave, but that they couldn't decide whether to abandon their child or to go with their spouse. Everybody had something to say. It isn't easy to describe those final farewells, the handshakes and quiet words of gratitude. Some of our good friends left their beloved dogs with us: the poor creatures understood perfectly well that something bad was happening, they whimpered sadly and wouldn't eat.

People rushed into the pharmacy out of breath, to ask for Luminal to tranquillise their children so they could carry them out in rucksacks as luggage, or take them to hiding places, unwilling or unable to go to the barracks for various reasons. We handed out cough medicine.

Many children later owed their lives to Luminal and codeine. That day quite a few people managed to get across to the Aryan side.

The ghetto gate was opened and the first groups of people left. The Germans kept watch at the gate to make sure no children came through. Any children they noticed were violently torn from their parents' arms. If a father or mother tried to stay behind with their child, they moved it away and herded the parents out. The children stood for ages at the barbed wire fence and watched with tear-filled eyes as the grown-ups departed.

Now and then, new details would reach us — that so-and-so had been killed there, so-and-so had been beaten to a pulp here, or that they were shooting patients in the hospitals. Two Gestapo officers, Hujar and Frommer, came to the fore during the liquidation. Hujar was a fat, red-faced creature who was forever eating apples, and who frenziedly shot at anyone he could. Frommer carried out operations by himself, by contrast with Hujar, who was excited by the sight or close presence of his boss, Amon Göth. Like a grovelling dog, he hung around his master with his eyes lowered and a revolver in his fat hand, reading his thoughts and orders from his expression. It was these two inherently sadistic men who were picking children out of the packed crowd of people leaving the ghetto and brutally tearing them from their parents' embrace. In every case the parents were cruelly beaten and the children, crying and terrified of the furiously screaming Germans, ran away and hid in the doorways of nearby buildings. After a while, many of them returned to the barbed wire fence and watched the lines of adults waiting to depart. The poor things stood there, their little hands gripping the barbed wire, with tears of indescribable pain and fear running down their cheeks as their little mouths whispered: "Mummy, daddy, don't go. Don't leave me here, take me with you".

Some of our close friends refused to leave the ghetto during the liquidation to go and live in accommodation that had long since been waiting for them on the Aryan side. My colleague, Irena Droździkowska, had arranged a place near Wieliczka for Dr Leon Steinberg and his family. Unfortunately, he had delayed the decision to go there for such a long time that now the liquidation had made his escape impossible. Dr Armer and his family also had this option, and he took too long making up his mind as well. If you had somewhere suitable to go, running away was less risky than going to the Płaszów camp. Despite this, the urge to stay together, among friends facing a similar fate, was often stronger.

It was late afternoon when the last residents of ghetto A left for Płaszów. The OD, Gutter and several members of the Judenrat had to stay behind until the liquidation had been carried out fully. At the last moment, Dr Weichert was saved from having to go to the barracks because the General Government's Department for

Social Care had ordered him to stay in the ghetto to continue running the JUS.

The streets, houses and courtyards, which until recently had been ringing with the sound of voices, were suddenly empty. The deserted houses, open windows and lifeless streets were a haunting reminder for those still there.

At a steady pace, German guards patrolled the border area between the barbed wire fences which separated ghetto A from ghetto B.

The streets in ghetto B were empty, too. People were hiding in the empty tenement buildings and nobody was brave enough to come out: showing yourself or leaning out a window meant certain death. The Germans were just lying in wait for such an opportunity. Now and then shots fired by the German patrols shattered the silence. I looked out the window and saw a German standing just behind the barbed wire in front of my pharmacy, aiming his rifle somewhere near my windows. I stepped back and a shot rang out. I heard the crash of a gate closing, snatches of speech, and footsteps approaching. Soon after, a group of people were carrying a wounded person along the corridor that lead to the pharmacy. I opened the door and saw that it was a woman in her mid-forties, her face as white as a sheet. She was the mother of five children, all of them still minors. Her husband had been deported in June and she had been left alone with the children, without permission to stay in the ghetto. She had gone into hiding during each operation and managed to survive until that day. "And even this won't break me," she said, "it's just bad luck, just at the time when I need to stay strong." She had been trying to run from one building to another, where she had hidden her children in the attic. The German had suddenly spotted her and fired, and she was seriously injured in the shoulder blade. It must have been a dum-dum bullet because her shoulder was ripped to shreds. The hole in her back was the size of a baby's head. She wasn't groaning, but was still in shock; for now she felt no pain, just weakness. We dressed the wound, even though the cloth of her dress was stuck deep into it. Fortunately, a few minutes later the OD's doctor, the kindly Dr Armer, came to our assistance. He finished the dressing and gave her an injection. The woman was hopeful that everything would be all right. She had to live. "I must save my children," she said, and then asked how long it would take for the wound to heal. We consoled her by telling her she would be better in a few days, but we knew it was very doubtful she'd survive at all in such conditions. We never did hear what happened to her. More than likely she and her children were shot.

While it was being emptied, many people chose a novel and ingenious way to escape from the ghetto, but it was also extremely dangerous. After opening hatches leading into the main sewer they descended into the rat-infested sewers beneath the streets of Podgórze. Laden with belongings, and sometimes with children in their arms, they waded through faeces which came up to their waists, sometimes higher.

There were two of these sewers: one at the intersection of Józefińska Street and Krakus Street, and another at the intersection of Józefińska Street and Węgierska Street.

Old and young, women and children escaped this way, and if they hadn't been betrayed, this route could have saved many others too. One of the first people to go down into the sewer was Dr Aleksandrowicz; the ghastly journey in pitch darkness took him and his family several hours. At the end of the sewer there was a large outlet on the river Vistula, near a railway bridge.

I remember that day as if no time had passed. Julek Aleksandrowicz burst into the pharmacy and told me about his escape plan, which he was just about to put into action. He handed me a thick file containing his academic work and asked if I could keep it safe for him. A final handshake, a final kiss, with tears in our eyes and… it was so very sad. He described his escape from the ghetto, and what happened to his family after that, in his book *Pages from Dr Twardy's Diary*, which was published by Wydawnictwo Literackie in 1962.

A long time after, someone came along with a letter of authorisation to fetch Aleksandrowicz's file (after all these years, I can't remember who). As I handed over Julek's work, I asked how the doctor was doing. I was informed that he was dead, that he had been shot. From the way the man winked as he told me this news, I understood perfectly what it meant — this was to be the official line about Dr Aleksandrowicz until the end of the occupation.

The first daredevils were successful. The coast was clear, there were no Germans posted in the vicinity. But this didn't last long. Betrayal was to follow hard on the heels of would-be escapees. Reports of escaping Jews travelled along telephone wires to the German police, and shortly afterwards they stationed policemen at the sewer outlet. The next escapees fell straight into the Germans' hands. In many cases, the Germans shot them as they emerged from the opening, killing them on the spot.

The night of 13–14 March was a terrible one. Ghetto A had been completely liquidated and all our friends and acquaintances had gone. As we said farewell, they advised us to get away from the ghetto because the Germans might eliminate us as inconvenient witnesses. In ghetto B, people were terrified about what would happen the next day. Nobody was under any illusion about the fate of those who remained. After all, they were unemployed and therefore of no use to the Germans, especially the women and children. No one slept a wink that night. People wandered the hallways, cellars and attics of the buildings on Zgoda Square as if walking in their sleep, and when dawn broke, the square filled with people once more, just as it had during previous deportations. Haggard, unshaven and unwashed figures emerged from the buildings; they had a deranged look in their eyes, expressing fear and resignation. The women came out holding children by the hand, or in prams. The old men came with velvet-bound prayer books and ceremonial robes tucked under their arms. Other children came on their own, holding hands. It was a beautiful day, warm and sunny, so they calmly sat down on the asphalt, laughing, fighting and grabbing one another's toys, then crying again. The crowd was growing, the square was becoming more and more packed. Piles of bundles and packages containing bedding, pots, pans and dishes grew next to the waiting crowd — they were clearly expecting a long journey.

I am often asked by my Polish friends if the Jews were so blind that they didn't realise what lay ahead of them. Deportation meant certain death, so why did they take all those things? Why did they add to their troubles on this last journey? Why didn't they have an instinct to defend themselves? Why did they allow themselves to be led like lambs to the slaughter? Only people who weren't there, and who didn't witness these events at first hand, can ask such questions, because they do not have a complete picture of what it was like.

Those without first-hand experience of these terrifying scenes cannot begin to comprehend the circumstances in which the people in the ghetto lived; they cannot understand the perfidious lies that were used to deceive them on the eve of their deaths. If only each of my Polish friends had spent even a few hours in the atmosphere in which the "actions" took place, where at every few paces somebody was being killed, beaten or manhandled, somebody was being bullied, if he could have known what was happening backstage and seen the perpetrators of these crimes and the methods they employed to intensify fear and create terror — one minute cruelly shooting people, the next fooling them with the hope that the deportees were going to live, and then the next threatening to take revenge on people's families for wanting to escape, commit sabotage or show any other instinct for self-defence — he would not ask the question "why". Besides, the location of the Krakow ghetto — in contrast to the Warsaw ghetto, for example — did not at all lend itself to major defence operations. It was squeezed into an area comprising a dozen or so streets. German patrols circulated around these streets and had a crystal clear view of what was happening inside the ghetto; such conditions did not allow for large-scale resistance operations or armed riots. Also, in order to ensure their own safety, the Germans prepared well for every deportation operation: they brought in large numbers of fully-armed police units which were authorised to shoot whomever and whenever they pleased.

And finally, there was the faint hope of survival which flickered in the soul of every ghetto resident. Survival — in those days that was a powerful word; can there be anything more powerful than the words freedom and endurance amid such terrible captivity, as death reaped a bloody harvest? This hope worked miracles: it gave people superhuman strength and staying power, and told them to grit their teeth and swallow bitter doses of humiliation. The urge to survive, not the fear of death, was the dominant trait. This is my impression of those times and those people, based upon my own experiences of the ghetto.

I endeavoured to empathise and to understand the mentality of the individuals and whole groups of people I encountered at that time, and I am now convinced that if things had been different, all those people who were shot at would have begged for mercy, demeaned themselves or attempted to escape. Those would have been the undeniable manifestations of fear and cowardice. There was none of that in the Krakow ghetto. I did not hear any pleading, I did not see any crying. The people looked calmly and resignedly into the eyes of death, but they did so with pride. The Germans failed to see their victims cringing and begging for mercy.

SS and Sonderdienst units entered through the gate at Zgoda Square and formed a double row. These tall, well-built sons of the "heroic" Herrenvolk were all fully equipped with helmets and rifles. Various dignitaries entered the ghetto in cars. The soldiers put their rifles in a stack in front of them. The ghetto looked like a town preparing for battle. The images which moved before our eyes were similar to those from previous operations, but with one difference: this time the killing was more widespread, as if the Germans wanted to satisfy their appetite for blood, to gorge themselves on it. From early in the morning, we heard uninterrupted gunfire: those with guns shot as they pleased.

With a sneer on his puffy face, Oberscharführer Albert Hujar furiously burst into the main hospital on

Józefińska Street and began shooting at anyone he came across, at any patient. Like the Grim Reaper, he ran through the building, from the ground floor to the attic, leaving a trail of blood and corpses in his wake. At the entrance he killed the porter and the porter's dog which, terrified by the shots, had hidden in its kennel. He burst into each hospital ward in turn, killing everyone in their beds and anyone he met in the corridors. He ran into the cell which housed the sick prisoners transferred from the OD jail, and shot them all, even though many of them were strong enough to go to Płaszów.

In one ward the crazed Hujar found a pretty young woman lying in bed. Dr Katia Blau stood beside her, unwilling to leave her friend, Dr Bergerowa, alone. Bergerowa had tried to escape through the sewers. Carrying her small son Fredzio, she had had an unlucky fall and broken her leg. A German had run up to her and torn the child from her arms; she would never see him again. Groaning in excruciating pain and despair, she had held out her arms, like Niobe on losing her sons, then seemed to mutter something before passing out. She had been taken to the hospital, where she hadn't been abandoned by the devoted Dr Blau, a beautiful fair-haired woman with light blue eyes. One can only imagine what those women must have gone through as they heard the shots and the footsteps approaching their room.

As if in a trance, Hujar stood and stared at them, shifting his piercing gaze from one woman to the other, and then moved slowly towards them, his primed revolver behind his back. When he was close enough, he hissed furiously at the seated Dr Blau, ordering her to get up and turn to face the other way. Dr Blau knew perfectly well that her life was lost, but she also knew she would win the battle — as a woman, a doctor, and a human being, she would emerge the victor.

"Shoot me, then, I'm not afraid of death" — those were her last words. He fired. And then something strange happened: Dr Blau's death saved her friend's life. The German did not shoot Bergerowa. He put his gun away and ordered a nearby OD man to have the patient transferred to the hospital at Płaszów. Not long after, mentally broken, Bergerowa took her own life. The loss of her beloved son had been an unbearable blow.

Two more doctors, Dr Jan Fischer and Dr Bruno Palin, were murdered in that bloody assault on the hospital. After the hospital was closed down, the doctors who were still alive were transported to the Płaszów camp. Some time later, we found out that Dr Władysław Sztencel had been shot at Płaszów, and that Dr Stanisław Eibenschutz had been put on one of the transports to Bełżec: there he was cremated in the camp's furnaces.

We also received news that two well-known engineers from the ghetto, Grünberg and Morgenstein, who had been actively involved in every construction project within the ghetto (such as alterations to the hospital and demarcation of the ever-changing ghetto boundaries), had been killed on Göth's orders.

More and more people, driven from their homes, came running onto the square. The Germans pulled them from a variety of hiding places, from attics and cellars. Not every German policeman shot them the moment they found them: the victims had to be thoroughly tormented before sharing the fate of the others. On the square, the Germans were shooting, beating and harassing people, but now they were keeping to a plan. People with documents issued in a foreign country, who until then had been allowed to roam free in the ghetto, and also the ones jailed at the OD prison, were being shot in the blind alley which led from Zgoda Square to the hospital for infectious diseases. I saw a small, thin Jew with a beard run into the square, holding some documents. He was a Hungarian citizen known in the ghetto for selling Star of David armbands, who though free to move around the ghetto had not taken advantage of this privilege, but in spite of the orders in force he had refused to shave off his beard. The Germans kicked and pushed him to the ground, then he got up, and then fell again. He waved his papers in the direction of the SS officer, and stood in front of him. The officer took the documents and, without reading them, tore them to pieces. Then he told the Jew to turn around and pointed him towards the alley; at its corner, a revolver shot in the back of the head killed him on the spot. Many people were killed in that alley. Against the wall of the building opposite my windows, they lined up elderly Jews and shot them. They were mostly people who had been pulled from their hiding places. On another corner of the square, they were shooting children. Even when it came to murder, the Germans were rigorously systematic. We saw a group of a dozen or so old women being chased into a narrow side street (Wit Stwosz Lane), their German torturers punching and kicking them. Some shots rang out and we knew they had been killed.

People froze in horror — they stood there silently waiting for their turn; because, if not here, if not now, at some point in the next few hours the same fate was in store for them.

On Józefińska Street the Germans set about liquidating the Kinderheim. They loaded the children into trucks. Babies were thrown into baskets several at a time, and then loaded into the trucks. Older children were led to the square, where they were shot at the corner of the alley.

And amid the constant selection and segregation of the young, stronger-looking children, amid the endless beatings and shootings, the tall SS and Gestapo dignitaries calmly strolled around and chatted to one another. Sturmbannführer Haase reigned supreme, surrounded by his staff. Göth was there, too. Amid the noise of unintelligible screams, whistling and barking dogs I saw Heinemayer, the ubiquitous Kunde, Heinrich, Olde and many other, unfamiliar Germans pass before my eyes.

The SS men began directing the crowd towards the exit, separating the men and women, and taking children from their mothers. All of this was done in a brutal, inhumane manner. Beating and killing clearly stirred up their senses, making them eager for more. They organised a race to the death, which took place right outside my windows, On the square, they pulled certain people from the lines, mainly aged about sixty, and gathered them together in groups. Then they ordered them to run as fast as they could. This was to determine who lived and who died. The Germans mocked and laughed as these poor souls were forced to run, first individually, then in groups. The SS men shot at them: those who ran quickly were saved for the time being. The SS men approached them, slapped them on the back and praised them for running fast, for being in good shape and having stamina — then told them to turn around and shot them in the back of the head.

In many cases it was the colour of your eyes, the shape of your nose or your facial expression that decided whether you would live or die. I saw a man of about sixty who refused to run. He walked calmly, without turning to look behind him. Cases of blatant disobedience surprised the Germans; a lack of fear of death made an impression on them and drove them crazy. They didn't shoot the man, but punching and kicking, they pushed him into the group designated for deportation. And that was their revenge. After all, they knew exactly what was in store for those people before their lives ended.

However, there were many people who owed their lives to these races. They were seen to be still fit for work, and were added to the group of young people.

They were put into groups of four to be transported to the barracks at Płaszów. Some of them left straight after they were selected, others had to stay behind until the authorities decided what to do with them. They were held at the OD prison until everyone in ghetto B had been deported and, as it later turned out, assigned the task of stripping corpses and loading them onto trolleys.

One hundred and fifty people had been selected when Göth reported to Haase that these people were able to work, and that he was taking them to Płaszów. After brief consideration, Haase said: "That's too many — reduce it by half". Seventy-five people were shot, the rest stayed.

It was almost time to leave. We knew this because they started taking away people's things. The Germans no longer deluded people about their fate. This time they abandoned the lies and deceptions — they were no longer necessary because the end of the ghetto had come. SS men violently snatched handbags and threw them onto a single pile. Here and there someone or other shouted that their personal documents were in their handbags or wallets. For the time being people still deluded themselves into thinking they would live, that they needed their documents. These reactions were similar to those of a hanged man who, though already dead, continues to twitch convulsively.

Trucks pulled up at the main gate. The crowd rippled and stood up, pressing their way through the open gate. SS men standing in the passageway were screaming like madmen, punching, kicking and hustling people towards the exit. The children's cries and parents' screams made our blood run cold. Children in prams were left to their own fate; their parents could guess what lay in store for them. The shooting didn't stop for a moment. More groups of Germans kept bringing children into the courtyard of the building near the pharmacy, and the bursts of gunfire left us in no doubt about what had happened. People were hurriedly leaving the ghetto. They had to jump quickly into the waiting trucks, or the SS men standing alongside would keep hitting them. Many people found it very hard to climb into the trucks, especially the women and the elderly. They were helped by their friends and relatives, who ignored the blows falling on their backs and heads. Most of them were bleeding and injured; with bruised faces and blood in their mouths, they filled the trucks.

Meanwhile, I witnessed the following scene: among the crowd nearest to our building there was an old woman sitting on the ground. She had clearly dropped with exhaustion, because she didn't react to the Germans who were screaming for people to vacate the square. She sat there, motionless; perhaps she had fainted. I watched as an SS man approached her slowly with his hands behind his back. How similar they all looked as they killed! The same movements, the same gestures, the same manner. With his revolver in one hand, he walked up to her, and once he was only a few paces away, he raised his gun, aimed and fired. I saw the old woman jump as if electrocuted, sit up straight and slowly spread her arms. Then came a second shot, and this time it was fatal. One more killed!

The trucks filled with people began to leave, and new trucks arrived to pick up the remaining groups. The square was emptying, and the liquidation of the Krakow ghetto was nearly over. Zgoda Square looked as if a bomb had hit it — there were thousands of bundles and abandoned suitcases, and here and there small children were playing on the blood-soaked asphalt. There were SS men taking the children by the hand and leading them to that horrific courtyard. Others pushed along prams with babies sleeping inside. Each time children were led away like this, there would be a burst of gunfire. To save ammunition, they shot several children with a single bullet by lining them up in a row. Several babies were bundled into a single pram and also killed with just one bullet. Haase tirelessly reigned supreme, accompanied by his staff. I saw Göth, Kunde, Olde, Heinrich and Heinemayer. The key player in the hospital massacre, Hujar, stood with his legs wide apart, occasionally wiping sweat from his brow. Frommer stood next to him, gesticulating wildly.

I saw the OD man, Immerglück, leading his elderly mother out to the square. In recognition of his service to the OD, he had been allowed to escort her in person. He wrapped a blanket around her, gave her final instruction for the journey, hugged her and stroked her hair. It was a long farewell scene: a lengthy embrace, the son's eyes full of tears, and the mother's filled with boundless terror.

As he slowly left the square, she stood there like a statue with her arms outstretched, as if wanting to stop him and hug him once more. The Germans were standing there, but somehow this time they didn't laugh. A few hours later, Immerglück stripped his mother with his own hands, and laid her still-warm body on the trolley piled with corpses. She hadn't been sent for deportation, but was killed on the spot.

Approximately three thousand people were deported that day. Haase reprimanded Gutter for not forewarning the authorities about the large number of residents in ghetto B. Some fifteen hundred people were murdered — SS man Hering reported to Haase that a thousand had been killed.

The ghetto was extinct, and one might have thought the final act in this tragedy was over. And yet the Germans managed to devise something even more repulsive than the methods they had used against the living: now they profaned the dignity of the dead. Once the last German units had left the ghetto, the OD and the Jewish detainees were ordered to strip the corpses naked and pile them in the gateways, then load them onto trolleys and take them away.

I watched them stripping old and young, men and women. They even took the clothes off babies. The bodies were piled chaotically on top of one another. How many times sons recognised their own parents among the dead, and parents had to strip their own children! Trolleys arrived in the ghetto and the naked bodies were thrown onto them. I saw corpses which had clearly been shot in the face with dum-dum bullets, because instead of faces there were blood-red holes amid blood-matted hair. Sometimes wounded people were thrown onto the corpse-laden trolleys. I saw a moving trolley full of corpses, and among them a woman clearly raised her hands to her face. I heard the groans of seriously wounded people as they passed through the gate out of the ghetto. Once fully loaded, the trolleys were covered with blankets before going outside the ghetto and into the city streets, and like this, dripping with the blood of the massacred victims, like butcher's carts they sped along the narrow streets towards Płaszów. There were several incidences of bodies falling off as the trolleys negotiated the bumpy cobblestones on Wielicka Street.

Every entrance hall left an indelible impression. Boxes, parcels and bundles of food for the final journey lay in puddles of blood. Religious artefacts — such as prayer books, burial shrouds and ceremonial robes — lay scattered, tossed about by the Germans in their hunt for treasure.

A deathly silence fell over the deserted streets and desolate houses. Every street and every entrance hall exuded emptiness. And from every back alley came a curse on the nation that had brought forth so many murderers. Everything in the ghetto, right down to the tiniest object, cast an accusation; every place where they had set foot was branded with the murderous crime and disgrace of the Nazi system of government.

During the March deportation, two well-known doctors from Krakow were deported to Szebnie concentration camp: Dr Paulina Wasserberger, a doctor who had worked in the national healthcare system for many years and had done a great deal for the public good, and her sister, Dora, also a doctor. Both women died during the liquidation of the camp at Płaszów. A few weeks after camp was closed down, we received the sad news that our well-known friends Dr Berta Silberberg and Dr Maria Pechner had been killed there too.

But it wasn't just individuals who were murdered during the destruction of the Krakow ghetto. Entire families, often numbering dozens of people, perished there; some of them had been in Krakow for hundreds of years, their names permanently inscribed on the earliest records of ancient Krakow. Their traditions died with them.

Great names that disappeared forever include the Holzers (bankers), the Wohls, the Oberlenders, the Rappaports, the Baders, the Eibenschutzes, the Wachses from Podgórze, the Schleichkorns (bakers), the Lachses, the Libans (who owned the lime kilns in Podgórze), the Parisers, the Hutters (who owned shops selling musical instruments and bicycles), the Horowitzes and the Frischers (who imported fruit from southern Europe). Then there were the famous Landaus (Rafał was chairman of the Jewish administration in Krakow), the Halperns (who owned the furrier's shop on Grodzka Street), the Aleksandrowiczes, the Wasserbergs, and the Blühbaums (who traded in Eastern rugs). Entire rabbinical families perished, such as the family of Szabse Rappaport.

I can still remember the Matzner family from Podgórze. They were regular customers in my pharmacy before the war. I remember old Matzner with his long grey beard and his wise sayings. One time, during a discussion about providing mutual aid, he said: "If you throw bread into the river with good intentions, it comes back to you against the current".

Perhaps the list of surnames I have given is excessive, and they probably won't mean much to younger Cracovians. But this list has historical significance; it commemorates the fellow residents of our city, the co-creators of its culture (both material and spiritual), its scholarship and its art. And being good Jews, they also were good Polish patriots who actively contributed to the development of Krakow and our common homeland.

If we do our duty to those who died fighting for our country by immortalising their names on memorial plaques, then perhaps it is only right for me to mention the names of those who were imprisoned and slaughtered in my memoirs. They are merely the known fraction of the many, many people who died; may those whom I haven't mentioned forgive me, but I didn't know all of them, not even by reputation.

The famous synagogue on Szeroka Street, which dated back to the second half of the fourteenth century, was devastated. It was one of the oldest structures in the Kazimierz district. The Germans thoroughly ransacked it, stealing priceless Torah scrolls from the archives, parchments that were hundreds of years old, Talmudic texts, and valuable liturgical robes. They took away old brass lamps and candlesticks, and ripped decorative sconces from the walls. These items were initially taken to the ghetto and stored in one of the buildings on Limanowski Street. They demolished the old "Bergel" building where, so legend has it, the great Talmudist, cabbalist, rabbi and philosopher Natan Spira gave his lectures. They thoroughly desecrated the old Jewish cemeteries, such as the one on Szeroka Street next to the ancient Remuh Synagogue (which the Germans had turned into a warehouse). They smashed the black marble gravestones featuring the names of founders, sponsors, famous philosophers and rabbis such as Bach, Jakubowicz and the Isserleses. The ancient synagogues now lay in ruins; these include the Wysoka Synagogue, the Izaak Synagogue, the Popper Synagogue, the Kupa Synagogue and the Tempel Synagogue on Miodowa Street.

They also destroyed one of the more recent cemeteries in Krakow, located on Miodowa Street. Here too they smashed up tombs and graves and tore out the granite and marble memorial stones. The large black marble slabs were later used to pave the garden paths outside the villas of German dignitaries. Two more cemeteries were also demolished to make way for the concentration camp at Płaszów. The cemeteries on Jerozolimska Street and Abraham Street were used as the terrain for the camp. Passers-by witnessed the gruesome events which took place at these cemeteries. As diggers ploughed into the soil, they churned up graves containing human skeletons, individual bones and skulls. The Nazis not only had subtle ways of destroying human life and dignity, they were equally good at desecrating the graves of the dead — something that is held sacred and ring-fenced with care within the culture of every single tribe and nation in the world.

These small examples are incontrovertible proof of what blind, organised hatred can lead to, and of just how low standards of human morality can fall.

It is often said that "the Germans were people, too" and I can confirm this; during the Nazi reign of terror, without fearing the consequences of their actions a small number of factory managers (many of whom were Austrians) went out of their way to help Poles and Jews, consciously risking their lives to do so. One such person was Juliusz Madritsch, an Austrian who was in charge of a factory making clothes for the Germans in Podgórze, which employed Jewish workers from the ghetto and, later, from the Płaszów camp. Madritsch knew about the resistance effort and tried to create favourable conditions for it. Not only did he get extra food for his workers, he also had trolleys of food brought into the ghetto. According to Dr Jachniak, who is an authority in these matters, the Jews in the ghetto and in Płaszów referred to Madritsch as their "guardian angel".

As well as the camp at Płaszów where, after the closure of the ghetto on 13 March 1943, all the Jews who had avoided deportation ended up, there were also the so-called Julags. These were the places located outside the main concentration camp at Płaszów where the Jews continued to work; from now on they were kept in barracks at their own workplace, each with its own OD police force, and never went outside its bounds.

My picture of the relationships which prevailed inside the Krakow ghetto would be incomplete if I failed to mention the workplaces located outside the ghetto walls which employed the Jews who went out to work there each day. There was a Julag in Płaszów, to the south of the main camp. The Julag in the suburb of Zabłocie housed Oskar Schindler's enamelware factory, where the Jews were treated humanely. This workplace continued to exist until 4 September 1944, and then it was transferred to the camp at Płaszów, from where on 15 October 1944, during the liquidation of the camp, all Schindler's workers (and many others) were transported to Brünnlitz in what is now the Czech Republic (Brněnec). Schindler remained in charge of this camp and saved it from annihilation.

The head of the OD at the Julag in Prokocim was my old school friend Lipschutz, a decent man. His superior there was SS-Rottenführer Ritschek, who liked Lipschutz and "looked after" him.

One day, a nervous Lipschutz came into the pharmacy. He spoke quickly and in a low voice:

"Tadek, today I'm going to stake everything on one card, it's win or lose. I'm going to escape from the camp, and I think I'll make it. We'll see! I'll let you know how everything goes."

"Farewell," I said to him. A last handshake, and he said goodbye to us forever.

Shortly after, Ritschek came into the pharmacy and took Lipschutz back to Prokocim. The following day we heard a rumour that Lipschutz had been shot while attempting to escape.

There were other Julags at Krakow airport and in Bieżanów. Dr R. Glassner, who perished in the Bieżanów camp, used to send me smuggled notes asking for medicine and for news of his daughter. I kept in touch with that charming man until his death.

CHAPTER VI

A GHOST TOWN — "CLEANSING" THE GHETTO — THE BUTCHERS OF THE KRAKOW GHETTO — THE FATE OF THE OD MEN — DECEMBER 1943

Once the ghetto had been liquidated, the existence of the pharmacy no longer made sense. After two-and-a-half years in the ghetto, I felt as though I, too, had been deported to the land of the dead, to a town utterly devoid of people, where the sound of footsteps on the lifeless streets terrified you, and where the very sight of another human being sent shivers down your spine. Streets and houses that had been teeming with people a couple of days before now stood empty. Death walked the streets, peering into every building and every home. There probably wasn't a room in the former ghetto that hadn't witnessed horrendous crimes. After two days of being forced to remain in the pharmacy, listening to the echo of my own footsteps, I went for a walk through the deserted streets of this ghost town. There are many people who have witnessed some extremely gruesome scenes, and many who have experienced horrific things, but there are probably few who have felt the same way as I did that day, as I walked along streets littered with corpses and pools of congealed blood.

It was already dark when I returned to the pharmacy, and the darkness seemed to intensify the eerie atmosphere. There wasn't a cloud in the sky and the moon was casting a silvery light inside the buildings. The empty, dark streets and squares seemed even more lifeless on the way back. Every open window and gate made me feel uneasy. As I walked, I heard — whether in reality, or in my imagination — the sound of windows being closed. Someone went running across a hallway, clearly startled by my footsteps, somebody lit a match in a window, then somebody opened a window. Suddenly I heard a whistle…and a slip of paper fell before me, thrown by a mystery hand. No, it wasn't a hallucination, it had really happened. Someone was still alive, hiding in those buildings full of murder victims, in fear of another human being no different from himself. I picked up the piece of paper and quickened my pace. The images of the previous days were still too fresh in my mind for me to calmly consider the content or meaning of the whispers I had heard, or to remember where all the mysterious sounds had been coming from. I met only one person on my way back to the pharmacy, an OD man named Rottersmann, who was one of my old classmates at school, a good and decent man. We silently greeted each other, not a word was uttered. At the entrance to the pharmacy, again I heard the noise of footsteps, followed by the sound of knocking on glass. I entered the building. It was completely silent. In the corridor I stumbled over a naked corpse. Once I was safely inside the pharmacy, I breathed a sigh of relief. I walked over to the window and looked out at the square, struggling to believe it had all really happened.

Zgoda Square looked strange that night, like something out of a fairytale about an enchanted city. In the moonlight, the barbed wire fences cast shadows across the asphalt, crisscrossing it into hundreds of little squares. Entrance gates stood ajar, and the windows were dark. There wasn't a single light, or a single sign of life. Now and then, dogs would run past like crazy and then disappear into the shadows of the buildings. It was hard to fall asleep that night. The silence and the feeling of emptiness were unnerving, and I kept thinking I could hear footsteps, doors creaking and someone tapping on the window pane. In the days that followed, I heard similar noises whenever I went into the ghetto late at night. And by then I knew I wasn't mistaken — it was real and not a hallucination. People were letting it be known that they were alive and in need of help.

The falling slips of paper said: "Please help", "Please tell so-and-so we're alive — we're hungry". But helping people was no simple task. The German police and the overzealous Jewish OD men could easily notice anyone who stopped outside or incautiously entered an empty building, or who communicated with those hidden inside. There weren't many OD men you could trust with the lives of people trying to save themselves. In any case, the Germans suspected each one of them of being a thief on the look-out for Jewish valuables, which were now the property of the SS.

But help had to be provided. I decided to go to two OD men I knew well, namely Rottersmann and

Grüner. I told them exactly where I had heard noises and showed them where I had found the notes asking for help. We did everything in our power to provide it. While the furniture was being removed from the hospital on Józefińska Street to the barracks in Płaszów, we managed to smuggle out several children. The adults joined a group of prisoners sent from the camp to clean up the ghetto, and later returned to Płaszów with them. This initially escaped the Germans' notice, as they didn't scrupulously count the returning prisoners. Later, when some of the people brought out of the camp to work escaped, it became much harder to do this.

In the first few days following the liquidation of the ghetto, I opened the pharmacy at ten o'clock, but only for a few hours. The Jews working in the ghetto could only really make use of it during their lunch break, and very few of them actually needed anything.

On the first Sunday after the liquidation, I was sitting in the closed pharmacy, reading a book. The street outside was completely silent. Suddenly I heard someone creeping about in the entrance hall outside. I listened hard. There was a gentle knock at the door and then I heard footsteps quickly retreating. I began to feel strangely uncomfortable. A while later there was a knock at the window overlooking the courtyard at the back of the building. I went up to it and saw the shadow of someone running away and then...more soft footsteps in the hallway. I opened the door, and there before me was a small boy.

Wojew. Komitet Żydowski w Krakowie
i Wojew. Żyd. Komisja Historyczna

Do

Szanownego Obywatela Tadeusza Pankiewicza

w K r a k o w i e

Wojew. Komitet Żydowski i Wojew. Żyd. Komisja Historyczna na wspólnym posiedzeniu w dniu 15.IV.1945 r. uchwaliła wyrazić Szan. Obywatelowi najserdeczniejsze podziękowanie za pomoc udzielaną Żydom w okresie niemieckiej okupacji oraz za głęboko ludzkie i nacechowane czynnym poświęceniem stanowisko we wszystkich, licznych wypadkach konfliktu z panującym w tym okresie terrorem hitleryzmu.

Prosimy o przyjęcie naszego podziękowania jako skromnego wyrazu wdzięczności i wiary w zwycięstwo ideałów humanizmu.

Za Woj. Komitet Żyd.

Za Woj. Żyd. Kom. Hist.

WOJEWÓDZKA ŻYDOWSKA KOMISJA HISTORYCZNA W KRAKOWIE

Kraków, dnia 20.IV.1945.

25. A letter thanking Tadeusz Pankiewicz
for assisting Jews during the war,
issued by the Jewish Historical Commission

"Please help us, Mister."

"Who are you?" I asked. "And where are you hiding?"

The boy's gaunt, dirty face wore a look of fear, branded there by what he had experienced. His family name was Teufel; his father had had a stationer's shop on Szewska Street before the war, and in the ghetto he had worked at the stationery Gemeinschaft. On 13 March his father had gone off to the barracks in Płaszów with the others, while the boy had stayed in the ghetto with his aunt and her small child. They were hiding in a cellar, where they had built a hiding place under the coal. They hadn't eaten for days, his aunt was very sick and her child was dying. They had been through some terrible moments — the Germans had walked past them several times, as they lay trembling at the thought of being found, or that the child would start to cry. Somehow they had survived, and now they were asking for help. I gave him what food I had and promised to let his father know he was alive, which I did. A few days later, his aunt joined the group working in the ghetto and got outside to Płaszów, while the boy managed to get there by hiding himself in a cupboard from the hospital when they were moving furniture. The smaller child died.

Time raced on. Gradually sparks of new life began to appear in the ghost town. New German chiefs were put in charge of the ghetto, with the aim of conducting the planned seizure and utilisation of the property left by the Jews. Unterscharführer Hering, SS-Rottenführer Ritschek, Rottenführer Zugsberger and Untersturm-

26. Alex Ben Zvi, first secretary to the Israeli Embassy,
presenting Tadeusz Pankiewicz
with the Yad Vashem medal in 1986. Photo by Jerry Bergman.

führer Balb were some of the figures who appeared on the scene.

Each morning the ghetto was populated by people from the barracks in Płaszów. This was the so-called *Säuberungskolonne.*[1] They were supervised by a *kapo*[2] and escorted by Ukrainians in black uniforms. After they finished work, they were taken back to the camp. More and more often I received night-time visits from people in hiding. They were sick and hungry and they came — singly, in pairs, and with children — to ask for help.

The cleansing of the ghetto began in the tenements adjacent to Podgórski Market Square. Jewish property was sorted and taken to selected buildings. Special workshops were set up, where items of furniture were fixed and restored on the spot, and a locksmith's shop was established to carry out repairs and odd jobs for the Germans. Despite Göth's determination to centralise all warehouses and facilities by moving them to Płaszów, a few workshops continued to function in the former ghetto. And there were many Germans who employed every possible means to prevent these facilities from being moved to the camp because they were worried they'd lose their jobs and be sent to the front. There were also large private businesses which were partly working to

1 *Säuberungskolonne* (Ger.), lit. "cleansing column".

2 A *kapo* was a prisoner functionary selected by the SS to supervise groups of workers.

meet the needs of the army, such as Juliusz Madritsch's company in Podgórski Market Square, the *Zentrale für Handswerkslieferungen* in the old "Optima" chocolate factory on Węgierska Street, which housed tailors, hosiers, cobblers, tanners, leatherworkers and carpenters, and Wachs' lamp factory on Lwowska Street, where they made ventilators for bunkers as well as oil lamps and stoves for the front. In time, all these workplaces were moved to Płaszów. Outside the ghetto, the SS created two enormous warehouses for furniture and for medical and dentist's equipment. One of these occupied two houses: one on the corner of Węgierska Street and Limanowski Street, the other on Podgórski Market Square; the other was housed in a large building on Wielicka Street which used to be a high school, where a large number of books were also stored. Items looted from other areas of the so-called district of Krakow were also brought to these warehouses. Once in a while, trucks would pull up outside them and the Germans would bring out furniture or medical equipment. Most of it went to the Reich, where it was given to Germans whose homes had been bombed.

The fact that these warehouses were located outside the ghetto provided an opportunity to escape. Many a Jew who had come from Płaszów to clean the ghetto took advantage of a guard's inattention and fled. Sometimes German policemen helped them in their endeavours — for a generous sum, of course. The Viennese officers Essel and Schubert, and the Volksdeutsche Wita helped, as did some of the Blue Police, whose guard post bordered the ghetto, offering favourable conditions for escape.

Work to clean up the ghetto lasted from 6 a.m. to 6 p.m. After that, the streets fell silent again, except for the occasional footsteps of Jewish OD men. Sometimes SS-Rottenführer would appear out of nowhere, on foot or on a bicycle, with his trusty dog, Rolf. Kunde and Olde were also regulars in the ghetto.

Still surrounded by barbed wire, the ghetto was guarded day and night by the German police and the Blue Police. Getting inside was very difficult, even for high-ranking Germans. You had to have a special permit issued by the SS und Polizeiführer on Oleandry Street. These strict security measures were put in place because SS and Sonderdienst officers were coming into the ghetto and helping themselves to all sorts of items, such as rugs, pictures, fabrics and china. The Gestapo and SS men working in the ghetto watched enviously as their colleagues purloined the fruits of *their* labours. Accordingly motivated reports were sent to their superiors, and the SS issued an order preventing any German, even those with permission to obtain such objects, from entering or moving around the ghetto freely. They would now have to wait to receive the items in a building on Limanowski Street which backed onto the ghetto. Without special permission, only Germans and their wives who were directly connected with the ghetto could enter it. The wives of Oberführer Scherner, Haase and others were frequent visitors.

One day, the people employed in the clean-up came to work in very strange costumes. On Göth's orders, everyone in the camp had been made to paint stripes and checks on their clothes, to make escape more difficult. They looked like circus clowns. At first sight it may have looked quite funny, but in this guise all these people, whose sense of human dignity the Germans had failed to destroy, looked truly pitiful. I must stress that I spoke to many people who were not in the least amused by these outfits; on the contrary, as if in defiance of their intentions, they prompted disgust towards the Germans. The Jews made fun of themselves and joked about their costumes. Even in the harshest living conditions, many of them had not lost their innate sense of humour. One of my friends came into the pharmacy with stripes painted on his clothes and with cap in hand, performed a low and courtly bow, saying: "Ladies and gentlemen! It is my privilege to be able to inform you that the circus has arrived and has pitched its tents at the camp in Płaszów. No tickets required, admittance will be given to anyone who approaches the gate. Unfortunately, getting out will be much harder — I do not recommend it".

I recall another friend saying to me that day: "It doesn't do me any harm. I find it more amusing than they can possibly imagine; and there will come a time when Americans will pay through the nose for clothes like these — they'll be showing them off as some twentieth-century curiosity".

Work to tidy up the ghetto was performed in a systematic fashion. At Płaszów, the workers were divided into groups which were given the task of sorting items of furniture, ironware, silverware and copperware. Bedroom furniture, tables and kitchenware had to be arranged separately. Broken equipment that was fixable went to the appropriate workshops, while items that were beyond repair were dumped in a square on Targowa Street. This was also the designated area for metal objects, which were mainly useless junk. The raucous SS-Rottenführer Ritschek buzzed about among the workers, with riding crop in hand. Only twenty-four years old, this sickly-looking young German hailed from the Sudetenland. The son of a third-rate singer, Ritschek was a habitual drunkard, a neurasthenic and a pervert. He suffered from a superiority complex and was consumed by the importance of his mission; he firmly believed in Germany's victory and let off steam by beating workers and robbing them of everything during his frequent searches. He was forever invoking the German principle that Jews and their possessions were the property of the SS, and that every German could do as he pleased with them. He worked people to the bone, meted out sudden punishments and threatened to have them shot. He saw himself as a thoroughly dedicated idealist who worked selflessly for no personal gain, while constantly pointing out the excessive greed of other dignitaries for objects stored in the ghetto. In actual fact, he took bribes, as they all did, and people were constantly having to buy him off and give him presents. He used to spend days at a time sniffing out thrills, and he would walk about the ghetto at night in civilian clothes, just watching out to catch a Pole breaking in. He would lurk in attics for hours on end, watching the tenement buildings which he suspected somebody might break into. Many denunciations of Jews who were still living in the ghetto because of the duties they performed were his work; he was also responsible for foiling the attempted escapes of several OD men.

Ritschek always behaved properly towards me and my staff, and he even protected me from the high-ranking SS men Mayer and Balb, who wanted to shut down my pharmacy a few weeks before the barbed wire fences came down. A few days before the Red Army's final offensive, Ritschek showed up at the pharmacy and demanded four thousand zlotys, threatening to kill himself there and then if I refused. He told me that money had allegedly gone missing from military funds, and that if he failed to square the accounts by a specified time, he would be arrested. It was also what he called a matter of honour, etc. I gave him the money, fearing he would cause me harm, which he was quite capable of doing.

About two weeks after the liquidation of the ghetto, on SS orders, at Göth's behest, all members of the Judenrat still living in the ghetto, and thus Gutter and Streimer, and the OD members Spira, Pacanower and Süsser were arrested and taken to the camp at Płaszów. At the same time they arrested all Jews in the service of the Gestapo who were living in the city. Thus the informers — Marcel Grüner, Diamant, Apel, Förster and others were taken to Płaszów. To some extent, this was an internal conflict between the SS and the Gestapo. The arrests of those working for the Gestapo were carried out solely by the SS. Despite the antagonism between the SS and the Gestapo, the two groups were in agreement when it came to killing the Jews. However, this was about individuals the Gestapo had specifically chosen for their own ends. In retaliation, the Gestapo tormented Jews under the "protection" of the SS. For example, Chilowicz, the leader of the Jewish militia at the camp in Płaszów, was arrested by the Gestapo several times. The Gestapo knew that Göth trusted Chilowicz, and this arrest was their way of provoking Göth and showing him their strength. Göth was forced to intervene, which sometimes ended very stormily.

Those who were arrested were placed in a single barrack at Płaszów. Presently, Göth came in and gave many of them a severe beating, and then told them they would be shot. When the Gestapo found out about this, they decided to get their own back by freeing the prisoners. This only made matters worse; however, the prisoners were eventually released. A few weeks later, the Judenrat's Gutter and Streimer were shot, along with their families. I recall there was some altercation between Göth and Kunde at the time because the latter had arrested Chilowicz; the matter was brought to the attention of Haase, who, as Göth's superior and Kunde's patron, was called to arbitrate. Haase summoned Göth to the OD building in the ghetto for a rather harsh talk. The entire thing was overheard by OD men, who repeated the conversation to me just minutes after the meeting had ended. During the rather loud exchange, Kunde goaded Göth: "You might be higher in rank than me, but there's another difference between us: because of this badge..." — at this point he pulled out his police badge, which was on a chain in his pocket — "...I can arrest you any time I want. You, on the other hand, would need to go to my superiors and obtain an order before you could arrest me." The discussion ended in a victory for Kunde, and Haase gave Göth a strongly-worded reprimand.

At the ghetto's repair shops, the Germans were giving the Jewish workers personal jobs to do for them. The locksmith's shops on Targowa Street (and, later, on Józefińska Street) were generally employed to break into Jewish flats or safes (which were usually empty), and then to repair them. The SS men also gave them special commissions to make artistic lamps, and this work was done under the trained eye of professionals, Adolf Giemski and Silberstein. They made wrought iron doors for Scherner's and Haase's villas, railings, handcuffs, and so on.

At Scherner's behest, the workshop produced three ornamental lamps from wrought iron. Each of them was decorated with thick rings, joining the curved "arms" of the lamp-stand. Before attaching them, the Jewish workers added a Hebrew inscription to the inside of each ring — a list of Scherner and Haase's crimes. They gave me the third lamp as a present, but there were no words engraved on it.

Then there was the well-known case of one Majer Goldstein, a ghetto resident who had left and was living in Krakow on forged Aryan documents. After he was betrayed by an informer called Cabaj ("The Gypsy"), he was arrested and taken to the ghetto for interrogation. During this interrogation, he claimed he knew of a place outside Krakow called Opatkowice, where there were gold items and dollars buried in the ground. A Gestapo officer took Goldstein to Opatkowice; there Goldstein found the place where the treasure was allegedly buried and started to dig. At a certain moment, he hit the Gestapo officer on the head with the shovel. The Gestapo officer collapsed on the ground, his head streaming with blood, and Goldstein dived into the nearby bushes. He sat there until night-time, and then got as far away as possible under the cover of darkness.

Up until the barbed wire fence came down in September 1943, the OD building in the deserted ghetto continued to function as a local branch for the police, the SS and the Gestapo. It had a prison and an office where the Gestapo interrogated Jews caught with Aryan documents or denounced by informers. This was also the place where they drew up protocols for emptying the ghetto, and where they produced reports about the so-called mood of the Polish public in relation to the political situation. It was where reports were brought in about Jews in hiding, and about Jewish property that had been buried or put into safekeeping. Now and then, prisoners were sent from the OD prison to Płaszów with an accompanying note to say whether the prisoner should be killed or sent to work. The OD building was where Kunde and Olde were based. Frommer often visited them there. Grüner was in charge of the OD prison, and the prison doctor was the kindly Dr Armer. The prison itself resembled a chicken coop, surrounded by thick barbed wire and lit by powerful floodlights. Prisoners assembled for roll-calls in the courtyard. Despite the zeal of the prison guards, there were still a few daring and successful escapes.

Kunde visited me almost every day. Whenever he was passing through the square, he would drop by the pharmacy and ask all the usual questions: what was new since the day before, what was the political situation, what were the Poles saying to one another. He asked me to be totally honest and not to view him as a German in uniform, but as a fellow human being. He assured me of his positive attitude towards the Poles, and he dared to make a few critical remarks about the German government, and about Frank and Scherner, saying that the authorities' orders infuriated him, as did the signs which read: *nur für Deutsche* ("for Germans only"). He actually attempted to give me a long-winded explanation for them: Germans did not consider the Poles to be *Untermenschen*[1], despite

1 *Untermensch* (Ger.), lit. "sub-human".

what the propaganda said. But it was widely known that Poles were able to ensnare Germans with their charms, and that they were capable of committing crimes which damaged their own nation. He said that the theft of entire railway cars loaded with food, coal and alcohol would be simply unimaginable in the Reich, as would bribe-taking, listening to foreign radio stations and divulging state secrets, e.g. concerning arrests or other operations. Kunde cursed the war and called the German politicians "idiots at green tables". He blamed English and American Jews for starting the war. He was extremely proud of the results of his work as Kriminalsekretär. And when his superiors asked him how he did it, how he was so successful, he would reply: "I never beat anyone, I don't shout, I speak calmly, and if I can, I promise detainees they will go to the camp to work, not to be shot… I always keep my promises and that's the key to my success". I took a risk and told him what the Poles were saying and thinking about Germany at that time. I assured Kunde that we were all certain the Germans were bound to lose the war, that we would regain our independence, and that none of us believed the English and the Americans would turn on the Russians, as the Germans wished they would. I told him that Polish intellectuals had been arrested and sent to camps, where many of them had lost their lives; I told him about the constant round-ups that took place in the streets and cafés, and about the extreme measures to which this system was driving the Polish people. In many cases, Kunde nodded his head and said I was right; he blamed the government.

Kunde realised what lay in store for the Germans if they lost, and said — half-jokingly — that he was planning to escape abroad. Whenever he had leave, he went off to the Reich full of black thoughts, and on his return, he would come to see me and describe the mood there. He told me about the colossal damage caused by the air raids. He confessed that, during his time in Germany, he had explained the hopelessness of the situation to his friends, and how defeat was in his view inevitable, but they had assured him that there was a new secret weapon which would soon be put to use. He then heard details about the weapon (apparently a friend of his was employed on its manufacture): it could destroy vegetation and life forms within a radius of several dozen kilometres and render the soil infertile for many years thereafter. This news restored Kunde's faith in a German victory. He shared it with me, but I had the feeling that people in the General Government didn't really believe these stories much. So I told him we had also heard about this weapon, but that we generally doubted its miraculous effects, and that we thought such stories had been invented to keep people's spirits up. If the Germans really did possess such a thing, it was high time they used it — what were they waiting for?

More than once I wanted to take advantage of my relationship with Kunde to help Poles who had been arrested. I remember I was asked to intervene after Dr Jan

Reguła, deputy secretary at the Jagiellonian University, was arrested. However, Kunde refused right away, adding that he would be honest with me and not mislead or give me false hopes. He couldn't intervene because the matter was not being dealt with in his department, and so any intervention he made would be seen as highly suspicious. If he ever could do something, it had to be in his department, and only in cases where the matter was straightforward. When it came to the Jews, he proved to me on several occasions that he could do what he promised. After the liquidation of the ghetto, old people were occasionally sent from the overcrowded prison to the camp in Płaszów, where they were usually shot, provided there was no note in their papers saying they should be kept alive, which very rarely happened. On two occasions I asked Kunde to intervene in the matter of two elderly women; he promised me they wouldn't be shot. And he kept his word. Kunde often did favours for my colleagues at the pharmacy, and he saved the lives of some of our friends who had been taken from the prison to the camp at Płaszów.

In the ghetto, the Germans' attitudes to each other were characterised — as far as I could tell — by deep mistrust. They feared, mistrusted or were wary of each other. When they were together, they were naturally polite to each other, perfectly unanimous in their praise for their bosses, and none of them openly criticised the actions of their superiors. And, of course, they all firmly believed that Germany would win the war. However, if one of them made a mistake, he would immediately be subjected to a torrent of abuse from the rest of them; he would be called a thief and a coward. I remember when Scherner and Haase were arrested for common theft and fraud, and for organising orgies at the camp in Szebnie, their subordinates were beside themselves with joy. All sorts of stories about the private lives of the arrested men went flying around. At the time, I asked what would happen to Scherner and Haase, and I speculated that they would be sent to the front. "It would be an affront to a German soldier's honour to have to fight alongside a thief; they'll probably be sent back to Civvy Street, that's the best they can hope for," came the answer. One of the many charges levied against Haase was that he had appropriated some paintings, including one by Wojciech Kossak.[1] I should add that the Germans were particularly keen on Kossak's paintings, so it was a severe charge. When asked where he had got it from, Haase told them it was from the ghetto and that Kunde had given it to him. So Kunde was brought in for questioning, but he denied everything and pointed the finger at Steinfeld and Brodman, Jewish informers who worked for the Gestapo and the *Zollfahndungsstelle*.[2] As Haase was no danger to him behind bars, whereas Kunde was still powerful, Steinfeld confirmed Kunde's statement,

1 Wojciech Kossak (1857–1942) was a Polish painter, renowned for his paintings of battle scenes.

2 *Zollfahndungsstelle* (Ger.), the Customs Investigations Office.

that on Haase's orders they were the ones who had given him the painting.

"You have to be careful these days," said Kunde, "because human envy knows no limits. There was a chap who held a similar post to mine, who once in a while would go to the bank to deposit such large sums of money that it attracted the attention of the authorities. Then, when he was unable to reveal the source of his income, they locked him up. To avoid any suspicion, I don't wear rings, my watch is made of nickel, I don't have a silver cigarette case and I don't go to restaurants or theatres — I don't want to draw attention to myself. If I want to enjoy myself, I do it at home."

Kunde spoke highly of Spira, Pacanower and Süsser. One time he explained the reason why a simpleton like Spira had been made head of the OD: "He was chosen for psychological reasons. If the post were held by an educated man, an intellectual from a different social sphere, he would have been completely out of place. Instead of doing as he was told, he would have complicated matters. That was the case with Dr Rosenzweig, an unreliable man who was unable — and unwilling — to fall into line". It was enough to buy Gutter and Spira new full-dress uniforms that would distinguish them from everybody else. Even though they could leave the ghetto whenever they liked, it would never have occurred to them to escape. All the Germans had to do was boost their egos and their sense of power. And that is why the authorities were truly outraged when Pilarzik, the SS man, hit Spira in the face. When Spira heard that Pilarzik had been reprimanded, his faith in his own power was restored. He worked zealously until the very end. Spira's interventions were usually effective. Many of those close to Spira were released from detention, or pulled from transports — all done to assure Spira of the special privileges that come with loyal service. Towards the end, Spira found out for himself that it was all just a sham.

Only once did I seek Spira's assistance. I went to see him in person at the OD building. Taking advantage of Kunde's absence, I wanted to see the Kesler family who were being held in the OD prison. The Keslers had converted to Catholicism many years before. Dr Maksymilian Kesler was the manager of the Commercial Bank in Krakow; strangely enough, he was able to keep his job there until 1943, and he and his family — his wife, son and daughter (who had attended a reputable Catholic School) — had been able to move freely around town. Until something sensational happened: one day the Gestapo pulled up outside the Keslers' home, arrested the entire family, sealed their house and took them to the OD prison. I had been asked to relay messages to and from the family and — most importantly — to implore Kunde to save them from death, which hung like an axe over the heads of everyone who ended up in the OD prison.

For the time being, I didn't want to ask Kunde for permission to talk to the prisoners because I couldn't tell him all the reasons why I was so keen to speak to them. So I went to see Spira, but he categorically refused. He was very sorry, but said he would never betray Kunde's trust, not for all the world. "It's simply out of the question," he said. His firm refusal forced me to speak to Kunde directly. After brief consideration, Kunde said he personally wouldn't have a problem with it, but what would Spira and his colleagues think. It would look odd, and might get him into bother.

"You know what?" he said, "I think you should go and see Spira when I'm not there, and ask him. I'm sure he wouldn't refuse you."

So I admitted that I had done that already, but hadn't got very far because Spira had firmly refused. Kunde smiled with contentment.

"I'm surprised he refused, but I admire his discipline. Yes, that's a man you can rely on. I'll let you see them."

And sure enough, I was able to visit them a number of times. Then I asked Kunde not to send them to Płaszów, where Göth was sure to have them killed. I explained to Kunde that I had known the family for many years and that Kesler had arranged a bank loan for me before the war, and that the money had saved me from ruin, so I personally owed a lot to Kesler.

Kunde listened to my explanations, looked me the eyes and said nothing for a long time. Then he changed the subject. Many days went by, and although Kunde came to see me every day at the pharmacy, neither of us brought up the subject. Then one day Kunde asked me if anyone had intervened for me in the matter of the Keslers. I told him no, and I repeated that it was my personal request, and that now I would very much like to make the same request again. As before, Kunde didn't say a word about it. But I knew him well, and it gave me confidence: if he could do it, he wouldn't be indifferent to this case. And I knew he could. I just had to be patient and not return to the subject.

A few weeks passed, and time was against us, but still Kunde was silent. The distraught Keslers sat behind bars waiting for news from day to day. Unfortunately, I had nothing definite to tell them.

One afternoon, Kunde came into the pharmacy. At a rapid pace, as usual without stopping in the front room, he came into my duty room, sat down, fixed his piercing steel-grey eyes on me and asked: "What's going to happen to the Keslers?" What did he mean by that? That was the question I should be asking him, not the other way round. What could I say? I asked him to intervene for a third time, and then a thought flashed through my mind: something was going to happen, Kunde's question gave me a little hope; he hadn't forgotten, he was considering what to do with the Keslers. In the moment of silence that followed, he studied the expression on my face. Then he stood up, said goodbye, and left.

A couple of days later he dropped by the pharmacy and asked me to follow him into my duty room. Once inside, he closed the door and, in a hushed voice, gave me the following instructions:

"There's something I'd like you to arrange for me as quickly as possible: I need you to find a Polish doctor to perform an abortion for a woman I know. You'll be required to pass yourself off as the woman's boyfriend. As I'm sure you can appreciate, this is an extremely delicate matter, especially as the woman in question is German. I'll leave the rest to you, I shall have nothing to do with the matter. This should be kept strictly between us — I needn't tell you what would happen if anyone else were to find out."

I realised that no Polish doctor would take this on, and under no circumstances did I want to pretend to be a German woman's boyfriend. So I came up with another idea, which I suggested to Kunde: we could have Dr Regina Fenigerowa (a well-known and highly regarded gynaecologist) and Erwina Order-Panzer (a matron who had worked in the gynaecology ward at the hospital in the ghetto, and then at the hospital at Płaszów) brought from the camp under the pretext of an interrogation; we would need a third person so that Göth wouldn't get suspicious. The procedure would take place in the duty room at the pharmacy; Dr Armer could administer the anaesthetic, and I would assist.

Kunde agreed fully to my plan and set a day for the operation. Everything went as planned. At around one in the afternoon, Kunde arrived with the little lady, and then skedaddled, saying that he would drop in that evening. By three o'clock everyone had arrived. Before the operation began, I told Dr Fenigerowa the whole story. She said she had guessed as much when she and Erwina were summoned to the police station in the ghetto where Kunde and Olde were in charge.

Everything went well. The ladies brought from Płaszów left, along with the third person whom Kunde had added for appearances. As it later turned out, the third person was a young woman who had been caught with Aryan papers in Krakow and found herself at the mercy of Amon Göth. There is no doubt about the fate she would have met. Satisfied with how things had gone, Kunde informed Göth that he would need to question this woman a few more times and told him not to send her for deportation. Like this, we were able to save the young woman's life. As it happened, she survived the war. While the procedure was taking place, both my colleagues waited in the attic for it to end. That evening, Kunde came to collect his sweetheart. He came on a bicycle. She was a strapping girl: she jumped up from the divan and, holding onto the bike with one hand, walked with her lover to the ghetto gate, where a taxi was waiting for them. As he was leaving, Kunde turned to me and said: "I'll never forget what you've done for me". As the door closed behind them, I felt the huge burden of responsibility for the entire operation lift from my shoulders. My colleagues came down from the attic and we set about some thorough cleaning.

Göth was informed that both Dr Fenigerowa and Erwina Order-Panzer would have to remain at Kunde's disposal.

Of all the OD men, only one had a bad presentiment about their future fate — Süsser, the secretary of the OD. With maniacal persistence, he kept repeating: "They'll finish us all off". He was especially insistent about this when OD men were not allowed to live outside the ghetto walls — even though the Gestapo had issued them with Argentinean documents and permits to rent flats in town. But when they found accommodation there, the authorities told them they would have to stay together in the ghetto as long as the prison existed.

One of the OD workers was Dr Armer, who joined the OD not long before the ghetto was liquidated in order to avoid being sent to Płaszów. He and his family (a wife and daughter) had Hungarian documents, which I was involved in collecting outside the ghetto. It later transpired that foreign documents of this kind were brilliantly forged by members of the RPŻ.[1] In Dr Armer's case, they were faked by Władysław Wichman (the former headmaster of a school in Podgórze), Edward Kubiczek (a painter and graphic artist), and Zdzisław Kasperek (who provided photographs). These men maintained regular contact with Ferdynand Arczyński, a member of the RPŻ in Warsaw who often came to Krakow.

1 *Rada Pomocy Żydom* (Pol.), "The Council for Jewish Aid" was an underground organisation set up by the Polish resistance to bring aid to the Jews in Nazi-occupied Poland.

27. The memorial in Płaszów
commemorating the victims of the camp

I decided to take advantage of Kunde's good mood and ask him if he could certify Dr Armer's Hungarian documents. After all, Dr Armer had played a significant role in the procedure at the pharmacy. Kunde was slightly taken aback, and he looked at me with those steely eyes. He was silent for a moment, and then he asked:

"Where are these documents?"

"I have them here," I said, handing him the documents. He scrutinised them for a long time and then put them in his pocket, saying he'd bring them back the next day.

And sure enough, he did, and as he handed me the documents he said in a low voice: "*Sagen Sie ihm, er soll sofort verschwinden*" ("Tell him to disappear immediately").

A few days later, Kunde saw Dr Armer in the pharmacy. When the doctor approached Kunde to tell him something, Kunde repeated his warning and left the pharmacy. However, Armer couldn't make up his mind about leaving the ghetto, and kept putting it off, until the final day came when the OD members and remaining prisoners were exterminated. Armer and his family were taken to Płaszów and shot.

One day something remarkable happened in the ghetto. Two OD men who possessed documents entitling them to travel to America were summoned to the OD building by Kunde. There they found out they would now be able to use these documents; after going through quarantine, they would travel together to one of the ports in the north of Germany. You can just imagine how happy they and their families were that night. They simply couldn't believe that, after so many years of hell, they would be free again — they could take their things with them, they could take off their armbands, they could leave the country! They were told to report the following day to the building which housed the old people's home, from where they would leave after going through quarantine. These OD men were called Ringel and Kerner. Ringel had a wife, and Kerner had a wife and child. People wished them good luck, and envied them, and there was plenty of drinking that night. The pharmacy, which for months had been deprived of a normal income, turned into a place of trade, selling vodka, sausage and cakes. In imitation of American pharmacies, you could eat and drink your fill at our pharmacy — we had everything from ninety-five percent proof alcohol to liqueurs in a variety of flavours. There was daily drinking, with some people even coming in for a drink at least ten times a day. But on the day Ringel and Kerner got their sensational news, almost the entire ghetto was tipsy. The following day, everyone said a tearful farewell to these genuinely nice and decent people. They left in a hackney cab loaded with belongings and nobody heard from them again. Just one card came from Ringel, which he wrote en-route to Hanover — and then we heard rumours that he had died suddenly. The fates of both men were shrouded in mystery, because all trace of Kerner was lost.

Another time the ghetto was rocked by sensational news of a different kind. Ritschek had a personal aide, an

OD man named Weitz, a German Jew, who advised him in every single matter, and whom Ritschek genuinely liked. Weitz's wife was seriously ill, a schizophrenic who suffered from suicidal mania. She tried to poison herself several times with Luminal, but on each occasion she had been saved. She visited the pharmacy every day to buy sleeping pills, and she used to tell us she was bound to kill herself in the end. "This isn't a life," she said, "I die every day; it's not true you can only die once. Everything that's happening all around us is so cruel — I can't bear to go on living in these conditions."

Weitz had quarrelled with Chilowicz (who, in turn, was well liked by Göth) outside the furniture warehouse on Limanowski Street. During the argument Chilowicz, offended by Weitz's indecorous remarks, slapped him in the face and threatened to complain about him to Göth. This was a terrible threat, as everyone knew what Göth was capable of. Weitz, himself a neurasthenic and a psychopath, was so distressed that he committed suicide that night. Ritschek went mad with rage, and threatened to shoot Chilowicz. Ritschek helped carry out Weitz's body in person, a deed which surprised the whole ghetto.

Weitz once complained about me to Ritschek, accusing me of hiding Jewish property, selling alcohol at the pharmacy, and of acting as a go-between for Jews working in the ghetto and their Polish friends on the other side of the Vistula river. Ritschek confided in Kunde, who emphatically denied the accusations. Nevertheless, he told me about it and warned me that there might be a search, not only at the pharmacy, but also at my colleagues' homes.

"You're lucky Ritschek came to me — if it had been anybody else, it would have been bad news," he said.

I thanked him, and a bottle of vodka and a packet of cigars put a happy seal on the matter. It wasn't the first time Kunde had saved my life.

From time to time, the everyday workings of the ghetto were interrupted by visits from the SS bigwigs, Haase or Mayer. The presence of the former on the streets of the ghetto caused a great deal of anxiety, not to mention the fear and terror prompted by visits from Göth, which were admittedly rare. Whenever these visits took place, everyone in the ghetto would hide away in tenements and workshops; nobody would go outside while they were there.

In order to stay in the ghetto, my colleagues and I were required to have our passes renewed every fourteen days, which Kunde arranged for us. One day, shortly before they took down the barbed wire fences surrounding the ghetto, I was visited by Sturmbannführer Mayer and Untersturmführer Balb. They couldn't get over their surprise: "What's an Aryan — a Pole to boot — doing in this place? A pharmacy, you say? What for? For whom?" they asked. After a cursory look round the place, and after opening a few drawers, they decided that I must close the pharmacy for good the next day. They explained that the Jews were no longer allowed to have money, so to whom was I selling anything? Ritschek defended me, saying that I also sent medicines to the camp, because the distribution office of the JUS didn't have any. But they left, unconvinced about the need for the pharmacy to exist. "It would be really bad luck," I thought, "to have survived for the entire existence of the ghetto, and all the deportations, only to be thrown out just before the very end. It would be more than bad luck."

Half an hour later, Kunde came by. I told him about Mayer and Balb's visit and about their order. Kunde asked me if I had shown them my documents and if they had read them. "Yes, of course," I replied. He left without saying another word. He returned an hour later, sat down at the typewriter and made out new passes, not for the usual two weeks, but for a month. This was his way of showing me he could do great things if he wanted to. He told me that he had used the following argument: there are lots of foreigners in the OD prison, many of whom are sick, and therefore the pharmacy is necessary, besides which it provides Weichert with prescription medicines for people at the camp.

Kunde's assistant, Olde, also made frequent visits to the pharmacy whenever he was passing by. Even though they were both friends, the moment Olde showed up, Kunde would quickly steer the topic of conversation away from politics. Olde was in his early forties and was one of the very few Germans who always spoke in a calm and quiet voice. He was born in Hamburg and was married with two children, and always avoided discussing anything to do with politics. Sometimes Kommandant Bousko would come into the pharmacy. He didn't like any of the rest of them, saying that they were unreliable, insincere and bad people.

And so the days went by. One building after another was vacated. Life in the deserted ghetto was strange, as if it only had hours left. Ritschek and Zugsberger spent the whole day running around like madmen, beating and screaming at workers. The exhausted Jews worked hard, carrying heavy loads on their shoulders, unloading items brought in from other ghettos and storing them in designated buildings which had been converted into proper warehouses. There were stores for stationary items, leather, linen, woven fabrics and so on. The people who came to work in the ghetto used a communal kitchen to eat there too. They picked up any foodstuffs left behind in the flats by those who had gone to the camp.

Horse-drawn trolleys driven by Poles arrived each day to take away furniture. It was stored in a building on Limanowksi Street and in the old school building on Wielicka Street, and was often transported directly to the homes of Germans. Meanwhile, the furniture and belongings of arrested Jews who had been hiding in the city was confiscated and brought back into the ghetto. There was a lot of trading going on at that time — people bought, sold and exchanged whatever they could get their hands on. Ritschek was often absent while these transactions were taking place, but he knew the fine details of every one, and what price had been obtained, money which would be going into his own pocket.

The nearer the work to clear the ghetto came to completion, the more frequently the Säuberungskolonne workers tried to escape, either individually or in small groups. A few OD men, having obtained foreign identity documents, pretended to be transferring to work for the Gestapo and took any opportunity that arose to flee the country. This is how Schleifer and his family made their escape, followed by Neiger and his family and, some time later, Türck. This particular escape could have had some very serious consequences, and the remaining OD men were scared stiff. Spira was livid, so angry that he suffered an attack of gallstones. When they informed Kunde about the escape the following day, he wouldn't accept the fact, but told everyone to carry as if nothing had happened. He was a most peculiar man.

At this time, by the special permission of the Sonderdienst, two weddings took place in the ghetto, conducted by a rabbi who happened to be working in the Säuberungskolonne. Spira gave his daughter away to a fellow OD man, and one of the managers of the SS warehouses, Demmer, got married to a young girl from the camp, who subsequently came to live with him in the ghetto. Haase, Kunde and Ritschek graced these celebrations with their presence. A few weeks later, young Demmer and his wife, together with all the other warehouse managers, were transported to the camp and shot. Not long after, the vast majority of the remaining

OD staff met a similar fate. For several weeks more, the small handful of OD men that remained in the ghetto were fooled into believing they would be able to live in town or go abroad.

By now, all the tenement buildings were starting to look conspicuously empty; meanwhile, piles of useless furniture and old scrap metal — often several metres high — accumulated on the squares, side streets and vast courtyards of the ghetto. On Zgoda Square there was a decaying stack of abandoned wardrobes, tables, dressers and other furniture which had been moved from one place to another again and again. One time, the Jewish workers were given just two hours to clear out the furniture from an entire building, a simply impossible task. And yet it was done under the personal supervision of Ritschek, who, in an apparent display of enthusiasm, told them to throw the furniture from the upper windows. Tables, wardrobes and beds fell and shattered noisily on the cobbles below. The items were destroyed in this unlikely way, purely to fulfil the stupid order. While they were cleaning the flats, the workers sometimes found valuable objects, which they sold via Poles in town. Larger items were put into boxes and smuggled out on the trolleys which came into the ghetto to fetch various things.

In the first few weeks after the Jews were taken to the camp at Płaszów, now and then the Germans got wind of a hiding place in the ghetto, either by chance, or because they'd been tipped off by their informers. Then under

Spira's command, whole teams of Germans and OD men went into action, assisted by workers armed with axes, pickaxes and iron bars. They uncovered elaborately constructed hiding places in attics, in cellars, and inside large baker's ovens, where people supplied with food and water could have survived for months, if not for bad luck or betrayal. Those who were found were first taken to the OD prison, and from there to Płaszów, usually to their deaths.

While the workers were clearing out flats, they occasionally stumbled upon the victims of poisoning or shooting, or people who had died of starvation or disease, as well as bodies that had been lying in cellars for weeks or months under piles of coal. On several occasions, the location of decaying corpses was given away by millions of flies. I saw corpses in an advanced state of decomposition. I saw the body of a woman who had died in bed on the day of the deportation — it had been lying under an eiderdown for many weeks or even months. Maggots had eaten away at her body, leaving her unrecognisable. I saw a child, a little girl, lying in her cot, probably poisoned by her parents when told they couldn't take her with them to the camp. In one cellar, I saw the hand of an old man sticking out from the pile of coal under which he had died.

The task of transporting the corpses of those who had died or been killed was carried out by the cemetery caretaker, Pinkoza Ladner (known to everyone as "Pinie Koza"), who was a well-known figure in the ghetto. He and his wife and children were allowed to occupy a small room in the Aryan district, in the caretaker's building at the cemetery on Miodowa Street. After the ghetto was liquidated, the Germans killed Pinie Koza and his family too.

One thing that stuck out among all this tragedy was the moving and proverbial faithfulness of dogs that had been left to fend for themselves after their masters had gone. Abandoned by their owners, they roamed the streets for days on end, looking for food. Once they found some, they would return to their homes and lie down under their masters' beds. I knew of a case where a miniature pinscher, the much loved pet of a doctor whom I knew, would come and stand outside a certain OD man's flat at the same time every day. The hungry dog would sit for hours at his door, but nobody could catch it. Once it had got some food, it would race home and sit under the bed, not letting anybody come near it, until hunger drove it back to the OD man's door. Finally, the OD man managed to catch the pinscher, and for two days he kept the dog in his flat, where it was given plenty to eat. However, after two days, the dog took the first opportunity to escape to its old home.

There was one dog that came to the pharmacy every evening. After some time, he brought a friend along for dinner. We tried to get them to come inside, with little initial success. We had to bring their food and water out to them. However, after a while they decided to cross the threshold and eat their rations inside the pharmacy, but immediately after eating, they shot out the door and ran home. Only one dog, a little French bulldog, instantly grew attached to us and stayed at the pharmacy for good.

From day to day, the number of buildings waiting to be cleared became smaller and smaller. The area of the ghetto also decreased, as entire blocks of emptied tenements were gradually excluded from it. The barbed wire fences enclosed an ever smaller zone. The warehouses were bursting with accumulated objects. Books taken from flats in the ghetto and from other ghettos in the Krakow district were stored in one of the houses on Józefińska Street, and later in the former school building on Wielicka Street. The more valuable German books were looted by the Germans, while the Polish and Jewish ones were sold for next to nothing to be pulped. These included beautiful editions of works by Polish poets, belles-lettres, specialist literature, and a rich collection of Hebrew and Jewish works, of both religious and secular content. Prayer books and large leather-bound tomes taken from synagogues lay scattered about in the courtyards, being destroyed by the rain.

We managed to save a dozen or so old Torah scrolls and other books. After the Germans left, I gave them to the Regional Jewish Historical Committee in Krakow, on Długa Street. I gave a few of the smaller books as gifts to my good Jewish friends. We concealed the oldest and most valuable Torah scrolls, chosen by an expert called Dr Armer, in precautionary hiding places, moving them, depending on the situation, between the attic and the cellar, until I got one of the carpenters working in the ghetto to design and build a perfectly disguised hideaway for them in the front room.

That was where we preserved the Torah scrolls according to the recommendations of Dr Armer, who said that saving a Torah scroll was like saving a human being. We had to store them upright, covered with an embroidered velvet cloth, and so they remained with us until the end of the war.

A few days after I had delivered the scrolls and books, the Regional Jewish Historical Committee in Krakow sent me a letter thanking us for all we had done in the ghetto. There wasn't a single mention of the Torah scrolls, nor did I find them among the many valuable liturgical exhibits at the recently opened Jewish Museum in the old synagogue on Szeroka Street.

Not a week went by in the ghetto without them bringing in Jews who had been caught in the city living on Polish identity documents. Each offender was first of all examined by Dr Armer, who was required to give his opinion on the matter of circumcision. Most of those arrested claimed that some years before they had had a procedure to remove an abscess, and hence the scar which looked deceptively like a ritual circumcision scar. In each case, Dr Armer always gave the same response: the scar could have been caused by circumcision, or it could equally be the result of a medical operation, and so he was unable to determine whether or not the person was of Jewish origin.

The ghetto also had some extraordinary days in the final stage of its clearance: the birthdays of Ritschek, Zugsberger and — most importantly — Kunde. On these days, gifts of all shapes and sizes came pouring in. The Germans were almost completely drunk and they left the ghetto early to continue the festivities in their private apartments. They even beat and insulted the workers with less enthusiasm on those days.

During the clearance, Ritschek would beat the workers ruthlessly and once he even shot one of them: the workers had been assembled in the courtyard of the OD building, and one of them had been summoned to step forward, a man on whom some objects had been found which he had taken while clearing an apartment, but had failed to report to the authorities. The sentence was passed and carried out there and then. Floggings were often meted out in the OD building courtyard too: twenty-five lashes on the bare flesh for any misdemeanour at all. On one occasion, Haase himself assisted in the flogging of a group of middle-aged women.

Any items the Germans deemed useless were collected and sold directly to the Poles who gathered daily in front of the barbed wire fence.

By August 1943 only the OD building and a few neighbouring tenements were surrounded by barbed wire. After 13 March 1943, the only Jewish establishment remaining in the former ghetto was the building at 2a Józefińska Street, which housed the storerooms and medicine distribution centre of the JUS. The JUS was run by Dr Weichert, a lawyer by profession, an extremely intelligent man and an outstanding organiser. Before the war, Weichert was one of the Jewish cultural world's most eminent representatives. He was actively involved in theatre: he was the founder and manager of an experimental theatre in Warsaw, and he also wrote several works on the study of theatre. During the war he was in charge of the JUS in Warsaw, and after its activities were extended throughout the General Government, he was elected chairman of its seven-man executive committee. He then moved to Krakow with his wife, son and daughter, and lived in the ghetto. As a mandatary of the International Red Cross, he handled all donations to the Jews.

After March 1943, the authorities gave the JUS permission to move into the building on Józefińska Street, where, together with his colleagues — Dr Hilfstein, Dr Tisch, A. Biberstein, S. Jaszczurka and Dr L. Leinkremm — Weichert skilfully organised deliveries of medicines and food supplies to Płaszów and all the other camps in Poland. Weichert was the only person who had permission to enter the camp at Płaszów (and the other camps in the region); he brought aid to the prisoners and constantly risked his life to deliver letters and money from Poles. Any letters or money that came to the pharmacy were delivered to the camp via Weichert, as well as the medicines and food which saved many people from certain death. As he went to bed each evening, Dr Weichert wondered if the JUS would be shut down during the night, especially as it was openly being said that they were building a barrack for the JUS in Płaszów. Dr Weichert worked closely with the RPŻ to bring aid to the Jews at various camps, and this aid even extended beyond the boundaries of the General Government. The hostile attitude of Göth, who couldn't stand the orders issued by the Red Cross and the civil authorities with regard to Dr Weichert, did not bode well for him if he were to end up in Płaszów. In July 1944, when the German army was fleeing in panic from the eastern front, the SS authorities decided to shut down the JUS. As soon as he was informed, Weichert and his family stopped sleeping at home, a precaution that turned out to be wise. Early one morning, a group of SS men arrived at the JUS building to arrest the doctor. Weichert's absence saved him from certain death.

The Weichert family's concealment and rescue happened thanks to the underground organisation known as the RPŻ. This organisation, founded in 1942, had its headquarters in Warsaw under the code-name "Żegota". In 1943, Prof. Tadeusz Seweryn (known as Socha) founded the RPŻ's committee in Krakow, which comprised representatives from various political parties. Its chairman, Dr Stanisław Dobrowolski (aka Staniewski), and secretary, Władysław Wójcik (aka Żegota), were from the PPS (the Polish Socialist Party), Anna Dobrowolska (aka Michalska) was from the Democratic Party, and Dr Jerzy Matus from the People's Party. Representing the Jewish community was a beautiful lady by the name of

Maria Hochberg-Mariańska. Many other people worked closely with the RPŻ, including Wójcik's wife, sister and mother.

The chairman of the RPŻ, Dr Stanisław Dobrowolski, hid the Weichert family in an apartment belonging to his sister, Dr Miklaszewka, who shortly afterwards took the family to stay with a friend of hers named Wanda Dwernicka, who lived on Zyblikiewicz Street in Krakow. They remained here for the rest of the occupation and lived to see the liberation of Poland. During their stay at her apartment, the Weicherts formed lasting friendships with Wanda Dwernicka. Dr Weichert's lovely wife, named Franciszka, a graceful and charming woman, and their son and daughter all tenaciously helped him to do his difficult job by making up packs of medicine and hundreds of first aid kits to send to the Jewish camps and other places where Jews were being held. Many people owe their lives to these medicines.

After regaining his liberty, Dr Weichert found himself in the dock for the fact that despite the instructions of the Jewish underground organisation, he had not suspended his activities. Weichert's stand on the matter was completely opposed to that of the underground organisation. Nevertheless he had tried — as he demonstrated to the court — to confer with representatives of the underground, to present his point of view to them and to prove to them that he was providing genuine aid to people in the camps. However, the organisation had refused to accept his attitude and had even given an order for him to be eliminated, though it hadn't come to that. The court hearing showed irrefutably that with the help of Polish and Jewish organisations, Weichert could have gone abroad or hidden in a monastery, but had not taken advantage of these opportunities. In court, he also proved beyond any doubt that the aid he had provided had saved the lives of many people. A few years after the war, the Weicherts left Poland and moved to Israel, where the doctor was warmly welcomed by his former students and friends.

Towards the end of his rich life, Dr Weichert continued his cultural and literary work. He published three volumes of memoirs and an extensive work dedicated to the JUS. He died in Tel Aviv in 1967. A fourth volume of his memoirs was published posthumously to coincide with the eightieth anniversary of his birth.

The final act of destroying what remained of the ghetto took place on the night of 14–15 December 1943. At a quarter to eight that evening, some lorries drove up to the OD building, bringing a group of armed SS men with Göth at their head. All the OD men and their families were loaded into the trucks just as they were, without being allowed to take anything with them. The inmates from the OD prison were taken too. They were transported to the camp in Płaszów, where they were all shot except for a Hungarian woman named Katzowa and her children, and Dr Kesler and his wife, daughter and son. Many months later, during one of the deportations, Kesler's wife and daughter were taken to one of the extermination camps, where they perished. Kesler and his son survived the war and regained their freedom. Kunde had kept his promise.

A few hours before the last residents of the ghetto were taken away, I was at the OD building, where I had come to see Kunde to intercede for the Keslers. Kunde's anxiety made a strange impression on me — he had been working in his office since early that morning, he was drinking vodka and constantly looking at his watch. He assured me that he hadn't forgotten my request, and he was clearly trying to get me out of the OD building as quickly as possible. He escorted me to the gate himself, and told Dr Armer to open it for me.

I said goodbye to Dr Armer, never for a moment imagining that he would be shot a few hours later. He was the victim of unusually bad luck. He had done everything he could to avoid going to Płaszów. When they liquidated the ghetto, he had stayed on as the OD doctor. By a stroke of fortune, as mentioned above he had obtained Hungarian documents for himself and his family. Unfortunately, he left it too late to use them.

The following day, they cleared out the apartments of the murdered OD men, taking away their personal effects. When Kunde turned up at the pharmacy, I asked him about the fate of the OD men. He stressed every word of his reply:

"They have all gone on an exchange to America. And make sure you tell your staff what I have just told you."

I wasn't going to let it drop that easily, so I asked:

"And Dr Armer… did he go with them?"

"Yes, he did."

"And did they take their things with them?" I asked.

I had seen the Germans taking suitcases full of things from the OD men's apartments. And again came the reply:

"They took their personal effects with them."

Now I had no more doubts about their fate. A few days later, everyone was saying that they had all been shot at Płaszów, and their bodies were burnt in a heap. The rest of the Jews in the service of the Gestapo met a similar fate.

A few days after the liquidation of the OD, all the warehouses in the ghetto were transferred to Płaszów. The barbed wire fence was the last remnant of the ghetto to be taken down, and work began to renovate the damaged tenement buildings, which were now allocated to Poles who had been evicted from the Osiedle Oficerskie district. A few weeks later, they knocked down the remaining sections of the wall that had surrounded the former ghetto. Apart from two small sections of wall, every trace of the ghetto's existence was erased: the little town that had seen so much tragedy was gone.

A new era began. The ghetto was no more, and the war came to an end. The survivors have dispersed to almost every corner of the world, but despite the fact that so many years have passed, our friendship with all those people with whom we endured the tragedies and the brief moments of joy has not disappeared.

after the June deportation of 1942
after the October deportation of 1942
division of the ghetto on 6 July, 1942: A — for workers
B — for non-workers
the maximum extent of the ghetto

28. The Krakow Ghetto — a map of the border changes after the deportations

A GLOSSARY OF GERMAN NAMES AND EXPRESSIONS

Arbeitsamt — employment office

Baudienst — construction service

Bauinspektor — building inspector

Blauschein — lit. 'blue certificate', a document entitling its bearer to remain in the ghetto district

Deutschland siegt an allen Fronten — Germany is victorious on all fronts

Deutschland liegt an allen Fronten — Germany lies on all fronts

Es ist gänzlich unwichtig, ob wir leben, aber wichtig ist, dass unser Volk, dass Deutschland lebt — It is entirely unimportant whether we live, but it is important that our people, that Germany lives

Ferfel (farfel) — (Yiddish) a traditional Jewish side dish: pellet-shaped noodles made from flour

Gemeinschaft — lit. 'community' (here: a crafts association)

Gesundheitswesen — health service

Heeresverpflegung — army provisioning

Herrenvolk — master race

Judenpass — a Jewish passport, a document entitling its bearer to remain in the ghetto

judenrein — free (lit. 'clean') of Jews

Julag (Judenlager) — concentration camps for Jewish prisoners

JUS (Jüdische Unterstützungsstelle) — a Jewish social aid organisation created after the Jewish Mutual Aid Committee was disbanded

Kriminalsekretär — lit. 'criminal secretary', a functionary of the Reich's criminal police department

Ordnungsdienst (OD) — lit. 'order service', a term used for the Jewish police force
Ostbahn — Eastern Railway, a term for the General Government's state-operated rail service
Rüstung — weaponry (here: a munitions worker)
Säuberungskolonne — cleansing unit
SS-Oberführer — a rank within the SS equivalent to Senior Colonel
SS-Obergruppenführer — a rank within the SS equivalent to General
SS-Oberscharführer — a rank within the SS equivalent to Staff Sergeant
SS- und Polizeiführer — a commanding officer of the SS and police
SS-Rottenführer — a rank within the SS equivalent to Lance-Corporal
SS-Scharführer — a rank within the SS equivalent to Sergeant
Schupo, Schutzpolizei — the Third Reich's uniformed municipal police force
Sipo, Sicherheitspolizei — security police
Sonderdienst — special service, a police unit operating within the General Government
Stadthauptmann — a government official in charge of a municipal area
SS-Sturmbannführer — a rank within the SS equivalent to Major
SS-Sturmscharführer — a rank within the SS equivalent to Sergeant Major
SS-Unterscharführer — a rank within the SS equivalent to Corporal
SS-Untersturmführer — a rank within the SS equivalent to Second Lieutenant
Untermensch — subhuman

Wehrmacht — here: a worker employed by the army
Zentrale für Handwerkslieferung — central office for craft supplies
Zivil — here: a worker employed in civil institutions or in agriculture
Zivilabteilung — civil department
Zollfahndungsstelle — here: customs investigations office

Compiled by Czesław Brzoza
(trans. Garry Malloy)

LIST OF ILLUSTRATIONS

Cover photograph — Tadeusz Pankiewicz in front of the pharmacy (during the period of the occupation); cover photograph and illustrations 2, 6, 8, 10, 11, 12, 13, 14, 19, 20, 21, 26, 27 courtesy of the Museum of Pharmacy, Jagiellonian University; illustration 28 from Andrzej Chwalba, *History of Krakow*, vol. 5: *Krakow from 1939 to 1945*, Krakow 2002, p. 120; illustration 29 courtesy of the Jagiellonian Library; remaining photographs and illustrations are taken from Tadeusz Pankiewicz, *The Krakow Ghetto Pharmacy*, Krakow 1995.

INDEX

CONTENTS